THE ZOMBIE GARDENER:

BOOK 1

BEGINNER CROPS

AS TOLD BY

JOHN BARRY

THANK YOU

Sometimes it takes a serious question to make you realize the humor of a situation. Thank you Marybeth and Susan for asking me about Zombies. Your questions helped me change a simple idea into a fun project.

A big thank you to family, friends and staff for putting up with me. All the strange looks, eye rolls, and the 'oh my god' smirks did not over shadow the heart felt questions and support. As Jessica put it, "you're a weirdo, but if the Zombies do come I'm heading to your house."

Thank you Bud for the cover art, one of these times we will team up with my words and your pictures.

Thank you Kristy, when I asked you to edit this project I'm sure you said yes before realizing it, at its bones, was just another How-To book. I promise you will get to edit the book of my fiction writings you've come to know and love. As soon as I'm done writing it.

I also want to send the biggest thank you to my best friend Paul. I don't think you realize how all those years of "what were you thinking' has helped get me through some very tough times, and helped me reach for levels I otherwise would not have thought possible. Thank you Paul, I love you man.

Contents

A MAN AND HIS FAMILY

Through the slats of the boarded-up window, the man watched the stranger make his way up the path. The man knew this day would come; he knew that someday he would have to defend his stake in this shelter, but he also knew he was too weak to put up much of a resistance.

He heard a muffled cough and turned to look to, what at first glance, was no more than a random pile of wood planks and broken furniture against the wall. If you looked closer, you would see an opening where the floor met the wall just big enough for his wife and nine year old son to squeeze through, to hide within the cavity. He allowed a slight smile to cross his dirt-streaked, bearded face. He was proud of that hiding space-- it was the first thing he built when they found the shack, and about the only thing that turned out right since he had the bright idea of uprooting his family to what he thought would be a safer life.

By the time he turned his attention back to the window, the stranger was already halfway up the path. He still couldn't make a face out; the stranger was wearing a floppy, wide-brimmed hat that cast a shadow down to his chest, his head bowed towards the wooden box he was carrying. What he could make out was how clean the stranger looked. The long denim jacket was faded, but clean and well-mended, as well as his blue jeans. His boots-- he had real boots-- were black leather that looked broken in, but far from worn.

He looked down at his own clothes, threadbare and dirty, his mud-caked sneakers cracked, and the soles worn down so much he knew they wouldn't make another season. He was so afraid of wasting water, that they hadn't bathed or washed their clothes in months. He was nose-blind at this point, but he was sure the three of them stunk to high heaven.

As he turned back to the stranger, his fear increased; he could now see a rifle slung over the right shoulder. He didn't know what type it was, but it didn't really matter. He could also see a leather sheath poking out of the bottom right side of the man's jacket, and the only word he could think of was *machete*. He rolled away from the window and leaned against the wall, trying to calm his breath and slow his heart. He looked at the cracked wooden bat in his hands and felt the fear trying to rise again. He had no real protection, and he was feeling sick and weak. There was no question that he would stand his ground, but for how long was another matter.

He flashed back to when he encountered his first infected person, a woman. She was naked and covered in dirt, which did nothing to hide the numerous scrapes, bruises and gouges across her body. As she got to about 30 feet away, still staggering in his direction, he could see that her breast, deflated and hanging limp upon her chest, looked as if they were chewed on, with open wounds oozing a yellowish pus. He could also see her face showed the tell-tale signs of self-inflicted deep scratches that all the infected seemed to have, as if they were trying to somehow release the fever rage burning inside their heads.

Her slow, lumbering movements entranced him, and he didn't realize she now saw him until it was too late. Within a blink her head snapped up, and from the bowels of where her soul use to be, she emitted such a howl of rage that her mouth stretched so wide the corners split and began to bleed. Startled, he stepped back a little too quick and stumbled, landing on his back, the bat he was holding falling from his hands and rolling away just out of his reach.

Before he could regain himself, she was on him, her face contorted in pure rage. Working on blind survival his hands shot up to her neck, holding her snapping jaws at bay. His only thought at that moment was to try and avoid getting any of her saliva, blood or any other body fluids in his mouth and eyes. A major effort with her spastic back-and-forth struggle. He soon believed he would lose this battle. The strength was seeping from his arms, and he had a brief moment of just giving up. . . when the bat banged against his head.

The struggling was so fierce they had moved almost on top of the bat. Reaching down, deep inside, to bring up any and all strength he gave one last push and knocked the woman off him. Quicker than he has ever moved before, he jumped up, grabbed the bat, and began swinging at her head. He had no idea how long he was swinging, but when he stepped back, his arms screaming in pain, there was nothing but a three foot wide puddle of bone and gore where her head use to be.

That was when he was stronger and fighting off an emancipated woman and almost lost; how the hell can he now face a well feed well armed man?

The winter months had left him and his family just about starved. They found this shack just as the first snow was beginning to coat the ground. He believed this is what they called a "hunter's cabin", a place to offer temporary protection from the elements, but not made for long-term shelter. The rusted-out wood stove still worked so they had heat, but the winter winds would squeeze its fingers into the cracks of the uninsulated walls and try to grab away what little heat they could muster. They melted snow for water, but food quickly became an issue. They were able to supplement the meat from the rodents and squirrels that found their way into the shack with pine needle tea and pine bark soup. He read somewhere boiling pine needles and the white inner bark of the tree would give you vitamin C. The tea was bitter and the bark hard to digest, but it worked for a little while.

He felt, more than heard, the thump; the stranger had reached the front porch. He pushed at the fear that was holding him against the wall and peered back between the wooden slats. The stranger was leaning over the wooden box he dropped onto the porch and rearranging the contents. As he peered through the slats, trying to see what the stranger was doing, without warning the stranger looked up. Their eyes locked, and the man felt frozen in place. His eyes were wide with fear, while the strangers were casual and curious. It wasn't until the stranger slowly smiled, his eyes crinkling into weather-worn crow's feet, that the spell broke.

He slammed back hard against the wall, holding the bat so hard his knuckles went white and began screaming in pain. He knew the stranger saw him, knew he heard him, and now he was going to have to fight for his family and try to hang onto this shithole of a shelter. He waited for the crash, the splintered wood, the rebel yell as the stranger burst through the door, madly swinging that machete.

There was only silence.

He didn't know how long he stood there: a minute, an hour, a day, his breath labored, hands aching, eyes focused on the strip of sunlight slowly moving up the far wall. He kept his mind blank, while he tried to muster up any and all strength he could. He knew the only chance he would have was to swing as hard as he could as soon as the stranger burst through the door.

Nothing happened, and the streak of sunlight reached the ceiling and began to fade. He became aware of a distant voice, at first muffled and far away. The voice sounded familiar, like he should know it, and it

seemed to get closer. He snapped back to his wife shaking him, calling his name.

"Paul, are you alright? What happened? What happened?" She kept saying, over and over. Then, another voice pulled him fully out of the depths from where ever he just was.

"Papa, it's food!" his son yelled from the porch.

A new panic arose and he bolted for the door, nearly knocking his wife over. He found his son standing over the box, a big potato in each hand, and a smile on his dirt-streaked face.

"There's like all kinds of stuff," the boy said. "Did the strange man give this to us?"

His body was still tense and in survival mode as he scanned the tree lines of the property. It wasn't until he was sure the stranger was gone, or at least at a safe enough distance, that he allowed himself to settle down. He kneeled down beside his son and looked into the box. The boy was right. He saw a burlap bag full of potatoes, a couple dozen carrots, onions, peppers, and mason jars of other vegetables. There were also small paper bags with handwritten notes of what plant and a date; seed envelopes.

He heard a gasp and turned to see his wife, her hands covering her mouth and happy tears cutting through the dirt on her cheeks. He saw beside her a number of notebooks on the ground and reached over to grab one. He flipped open the cover and began to read: *The Zombie Gardener: Book One, Beginner Crops*.

THE ZOMBIE GARDENER:
BOOK 1
BEGINNER CROPS

INTRODUCTION

If this turns out to suck, then blame the kids.

They're the ones who originally pushed me to do this. Giving me that line of shit about, "What if something happens to you?', and "Who will pass down this knowledge?"; and then sucking up with, "What if this is the thing that brings the world back?" It's bullshit, every bit of it, and I know they're just hoping to keep me occupied and not up their asses with chores. Then again, I think I need the distraction, something that will keep me out of the homemade whiskey.

The only problem is, how do I start this? The how-to stuff speaks for itself, but the kids say I have to introduce myself, explain how I began survival gardening. The issue is there was no defining incident, no real *ah-ha* moment to point to. I had an equal distrust of government and science, and a growing disappointment in my fellow man's ability to do the right thing. I also thought we were long overdue for Mother Nature to give us a bitch slap. In the end, it wasn't really just one thing, it was more of a conspiring group of whispers that turned into a yell.

It was that yell that first brought me to the Prepper Movement, which sparked interest in me on some levels, but not as a final blueprint for survival. It just didn't make sense to have 25 years of freeze-dried, heavily preserved food stockpiled. First and foremost, what if nothing happens, what if the fate goblins give the world another twist and all was right again with a peace that lasts 100 years? You're going to feel pretty damn silly you spent all that time and money on all that stuff when you could have had a cool-looking motorcycle.

But on the other side of the pendulum, what if the worst of the worst happens? Did I really want to live in a bunker for years until the air and water outside was safe again? I can remember times the family was stuck in the house for a couple of days because of rain, and by the second day we were ready to kill each other. Now you want me to do this for months or years, in a confined space living on canned goods and MREs? You've got to be kidding me.

The other side of the coin was the survivalists, except the only experience I had was seeing news reports of uniformed militants training in the mountains for the next Civil War, or that lone guy roaming the rainforest eating bug larva and drinking his own urine. Now, my wife gags at the thought of trying pickled herring, so I'm pretty confident bug larva and urine don't have a shot.

From all the books, all the television shows, on-line videos, and how-to magazines from both sides, I was able to pick out ideas that made sense to me. I was able to put together a "Prepping to Survive" guide, so to speak. I knew there were some items I wouldn't be able to hunt for or grow so easily, and began stockpiling those. I also knew that to have any type of sustainable living, I would have to hone up on my hunting, fishing, and especially gardening skills.

It was the garden that finally won the family over with the Sunday dinners made from things picked out of the yard that very morning. There's something about going from the dirt, to the kitchen, to your plate in a matter of an hour that can bring everything else into perspective. You begin to notice how real the stress is just going to the grocery store. You stress while driving around trying to find a parking space; you stress while trying to navigate in and out of those crowded aisles; you stress over what brand is the best value; you stress over the look and cost at the meat counter; finally, you stress when that 17-year-old high school kid smiles at you, and asks for two-thirds of your paycheck to cover it all.

Even so, the family was still at arm's length about "Dad's Hobby." Back then, I wasn't such the survival hero, and nobody was asking for my opinions. Mostly, I got the head shake, and the *he's gone off the deep end now* pity looks. Of course, the wife and kids rolled their eyes at me, but they all knew where the Bug-out bags were, and kept all my "survival" gifts close at hand. There were even family members who asked me in hushed tones, "Do you really think zombies are coming?" But, then again, that was before the zombies actually came.

My son asked me what I thought would actually happen, but there was so much going on at the time that I thought the better question would be what would happen first. Mother Nature was due to send us an ass-kicking storm to knock us to our knees for a few months; terrorists were getting better at bringing the fight to our homeland with these lone wolves popping out of nowhere like some perverse whack-a-mole game; and the entire country seemed on edge about everything, and incapable of doing anything about it. We were ripe for a good, old fashioned bitch-slap.

Damn if I wasn't right, yet again. In a matter of a couple weeks, a massive earthquake devastated the west coast, then two back-to-back hurricanes created massive damage up and down the east coast. Of course, record-breaking tornadoes joined the party to make sure mid-country wasn't missing out on any of the fun. The country was hurting and barely limping along. Now, either their timing was impeccable, or they took advantage of our weakened state, but these lone wolf terrorists chose this time to wage some strategic attacks that took out the entire country's power grid. This not only sent us back to the Stone Age, but shut down the entire medical network for the country. It gave the germs an opportunity to come out and play and three months later a rabies virus infected a third of the country's population, leaving most in an angry zombie-like state.

Only they are not the type of zombies we've all come to know and love. They are not the walking dead. In fact, they are very much alive. Or alive in the sense that their lungs breathe air and their heart beats blood; but their brain only functions at a basic, animalistic level. Don't get me wrong, they will eat you. They will charge you ripping, clawing and biting in blind rage, and if they feel pain they don't react to it. It is only after you are dead, your guts spilled out over the ground, that their rage subsides and then they will begin to feed.

Before we go on to the meat and 'potatoes', pun intended, I feel the need to have full disclosure. I have never been, nor claim to be, an expert on gardening, nor am I an expert on survival or killing zombies. I'm just an average guy, who through a lot of trial and error, figured out how to do a handful of things right, and these things are the main reason why my family and I have survived. Because you can no longer go to the hardware store to buy a bag of 6-24-24 fertilizer to increase the ammonium nitrates in your soil for tomatoes. There are no more scientific equipment to test the soil's pH levels, and no more bottles of insecticides to screw onto your garden hose to spray away the insects.

The old world is still fresh in our minds and can get in the way sometimes, because we can easily forget that all that stuff is now gone. Sadly, some still think the modern world is coming back to save them. All I'm trying to do is show people with just some dirt and seeds how to get as much food out of a little space, so they can survive the rest of the year.

OK, enough of this. Let me tell you about some crops I feel are a must for any beginner's garden. –Z-

POTATO

One of the more prolific plants you will find after the shit hits the fan is the simple potato. I won't bore you with the multiple varieties, but most are easy to sprout, need little space to grow, and just a two-inch cube can produce a few pounds of crop. As with most root crops, they are easy to store and, under the right conditions, have a long shelf-life which makes them the perfect post-apocalyptic food source.

If planted early spring, you can ideally harvest in the early summer. Then, with a bit of a boost to the soil, you can replant a second crop in the early fall that will be ready by the first frost. This should give you more than enough to get through a cold, snowy winter, or help you wait out the herd of zombies that have just made their way into your neighborhood.

The health benefits of a medium-sized spud includes providing you with around 100 calories, more potassium than a banana, and if you add it to a couple meals a week, it will give you enough vitamin C to fight off scurvy. It also contains calcium, protein, niacin, and B-Complex which assists in skin and digestive health, and has been shown to help fight against kidney stones. The muscle-heads always fought against it because of the carbs, but they're all worm meat now, so who cares what they thought.

As I said in the beginning, I'm not here to lecture you on how type A potato has the texture and consistency conducive to baking, while B potato has the density that best allows it for longer cooking in soups and stews. When your family is hungry, and the long, cold winter is peeking over the horizon, will you really give a shit what type of potato it is? Now, figure in how you're going to find all these types, since the days of variety with anything ended when the President ate his entire staff while locked in the White House bunker. When the world took a nosedive into the toilet, I had some Yukon Gold and some Red Bliss, and I have carried these two into today. No one in the homestead has complained yet.

I could go on for a few more pages just about the benefits of the potato, from sustenance, to health, to making alcohol, to even making a battery out of it... but, my goal is to keep your attention and not bore you. I'll end the summary by saying, why suffer with the salt and preservatives of freeze-dried survival packs when you can have a simple potato grown by your own two hands?

SEEDING

As far as I am concerned, a seed potato is nothing more than the last spud in your storage bin. Before the virus, back when grocery stores were open on every corner, most can remember reaching into that cardboard bag for the last potato and pulling out something right out of Alien Adventures. Kind of looked like a potato, but with these mutated looking limbs poking out of it. Those limbs are the sprouts, which will grow runners that the potato grows off of. The sprouts grow out of what we commonly call the "eyes" of the potato, those weird indentations on the potato. That potato with sprouts coming out of the eyes, my friends, is what is called a seed potato.

I know there are more than a couple of you scratching your head, still wondering where in the hell are the seeds. To make it easier, think of that movie from the old world in which a plant-like alien invaded earth. The plant would consume a human, than shoot out a vine in which an identical form to the human would grow. That, my simple friend, is pretty much the life of a potato. No, it is not going to consume a human, that's just a metaphor for... never mind, let's just move on.

If you store your potatoes over any length of time, you may get a fair number of seed potatoes to continue your crop.

You can also take a potato and place it into a paper bag, and keep it in a dark, cool area until the eyes begin to sprout, which can take anywhere from a couple weeks to over a month.

I can remember before the collapse of society as we know it, I tried this with a store-bought potato and my first attempt failed: no matter how long that potato stayed in that paper bag, it would not sprout. I soon learned that most potatoes in the general food market were treated with growth inhibitors to stop the sprouting process. I guess customers were less apt to buy a potato with deformed appendages growing out of it. I did better with a potato from the organic aisle, and then caught on to asking the produce manager if there are any seed potatoes in the back, ready for the trash. Sometimes, I got them for free.

I know none of that helps you out today, but there are some farmer's markets that have begun to sprout up in the larger villages, and I have heard word of some farm feed stores beginning to open who will have a number of varieties ready for planting.

PRE-PLANTING

Potatoes are so prolific that planting is more about what you have tried and are comfortable with, than a true right vs. wrong method. Some methods are a bit haphazard, with people planting the whole potato in a bucket, then forgetting about it for a couple months, to some success. If the grid hadn't shut down and sent us back into the Dark Ages, and we were able to run to the store for a bag of taters, then fine, go for it. But, I'm not sure I would play *potato roulette* when it comes to feeding my family.

The method I've used may have additional steps, but it has not only been extremely successful, it has also produced a larger harvest with bigger potatoes. Yet, as easy as potatoes can be, there are a couple things you need to keep in mind to ensure success.

The key thing to remember is temperature. Potatoes do not like cold or heat, and do best when the daytime temps are between 60° and 70°, and nighttime temps don't fall below 45° to 55°. Once the temp gets above 85°, the runners can stop producing, giving you a smaller yield and smaller potatoes.

This leads into the next thing to consider, which is when to plant. You need to figure in a grow time of 90 to 100 days into where you live to find that temperature sweet-spot. If your homestead is in the warmer climates, you should consider a February-to-March planting for an April-to-May harvest. Then, consider an October-to-September second planting for a December-to-January harvest. I'm in the Northeast, so my ideal planting is not until April for a harvest in June to early July, and I try to get in a second planting in late August to September for a harvest in time for Thanksgiving. It's OK if you miss any of these sweet spots; we are still talking potatoes. Those of you in the cooler areas can get away with a summer crop. You need to baby it with extra water and mulch to insulate, and may even have to provide some shade during peak heat, but you can do it. I did, and got a smaller but decent crop. If you're in the warmer areas, you have a bigger fall window so it shouldn't be a big issue.

Now, we need to decide where to plant. Even though it doesn't like heat, the potato loves the sun so somewhere in open sun is preferred. It also hates to have its feet wet for too long, so you need good drainage, and it likes a simple mix of compost and soil with some hay or grass clippings for a boost of acid. Potatoes are not a fan of manure-based fertilizer. They are also prone to insect infestation and certain crop diseases, which are best controlled by rotating the planting beds each year.

Because you didn't have the luxury of bugging out to a 10-acre farm with a 100,000 square-foot attached survival bunker, and instead have had to hunker down in a small ranch house with maybe a couple thousand square feet of usable backyard, all is not lost. You still have choices, even for potatoes. Of course, there are raised beds to think about, but I have always been of the thought that using raised beds in a small garden for potatoes can limit your overall garden yield. It's one of those debatable questions that will never be answered, because there are equally as many pros as there are cons to the question. As for myself, I prefer to save the raised beds for crops that don't need as deep of a root system as potatoes.

For a small real estate of garden space, I tend to use containers. Take a moment to think about it: every house you've scavenged, every shell of a store you've explored, every garage, every shed, the one common item you will see is the five-gallon plastic bucket. The damn things are everywhere. Preppers stored tons of food and supplies in them, only to get bit by zombies themselves, and when looters ransacked the WalMarts and Costcos of the world, what is the one thing they ignored? You got it: the five-gallon plastic bucket. They are airtight, watertight, sturdy, and will last the better part of a few centuries. I consider them the most versatile item you can have in post-apocalyptic times, and they are one hell of a space-saving growing vessel as well.

A five-gallon plastic bucket using less than a 6" radius of space in your garden can produce up to five pounds of potatoes. If a couple of good seed potatoes can plant four buckets in two 90-day plantings, that will give you forty pounds of potatoes before winter by using only 4-6 feet of garden space. No matter how you do the math, that ain't half frickin' bad. I've seen potatoes grown in trash bags that are rolled up and filled with more dirt as the plant grows, and I've seen them grown in wooden boxes, hay bales, an old bathtub, large urns, and, of course, raised beds for those who have more garden real estate. For myself, I do use the five-gallon buckets, but I also have a black resin tub that sits 4' deep by 6' wide. In a past life, it sat inside the ground and was used as a garden water feature. After surviving a number of winters, it developed a crack and would no longer hold water. I dug it up, drilled a couple of drain holes in the bottom, and this past growing season that tub was used for an early crop of yellow potato, then a late summer crop of carrots, and a fall crop of red bliss potato.

The best argument for container gardening is if this new world order of chaos reaches your front door and you need to bug-out, you can take your crops with you.

PLANTING

No matter what type of container you use, the planting is typically the same. Drill enough holes in the bottom of the container; half-inch holes work best for me. My five-gallon buckets have four holes along the bottom edge and one in the center, and this has worked out well. Place a couple inches of small stone on the bottom-- I try to use anything that is a couple of inches bigger than the drilled holes. This not only helps with drainage by keeping the holes from getting clogged with dirt, but also stabilizes the container against tipping over in a surprise storm.

You know, it's the small things you took for granted that you miss the most after it all came crumbling down. I miss picking up a newspaper, going on-line, or turning on the television to get a simple weather report. I try to read nature's signs, but have to admit that I get it wrong most of the time. Maybe in a past life, I really was a weatherman.

To give the seed a good bed to start, I lay down four inches of a good mixture of compost, topsoil, and a handful of chopped hay. Remember, potatoes grow upwards, so you don't need a deep bed for a root system, but give it a good soil mix to help it along. Now your container is ready for seed, and here, my friends, is where the debates begin. Plant whole or cut, how big to cut, let it age or plant right away, and on and on. As I said, the right way is the tried and true way of your personal preference. Anything and everything can affect the harvest of your garden: where you live, rainfall, soil, and when you plant. My suggestion is to not let any one method be your starting point, and chance not getting a harvest; instead, try a couple of methods together and pick and fine-tune the method that works best for you in your area. The following is my preferred method.

I'm a cutter and I'll briefly explain why. If you plant half or the whole potato, and all is right with this off-the-grid world, you may see between three and five sprouts. My contribution to the debate is that these sprouts will be growing off of one seed, compacting the space the sprouts are growing in, and nature has a way of adjusting to compacted spaces by growing smaller and fewer.

So, I cut my seed potato into as many irregular cubes as the eyes and sprouts on the potato allow. Nature is not perfect and neither will your seed cubes be, but I keep at least one eye or sprout and two to three inches of meat on each cube. Someone once told me to keep the cubes to 2 ounces each, but let's see a show of hands on who can look at a piece of potato and tell if it's 2 ounces... *(insert sound of crickets here)*.

The freshly-cut potato brings us to the next stage of debate: Do I plant, or do I cure? Again, there is no definitive answer, but I pose a simple question: If your hand were suddenly cut off, would you shove the bloody stump into wet dirt and hope the wound heals before disease and rot sets in?

No? Then why do it to an important food source? As soon as you cut into the potato, enzymes begin working on producing a protective film over the exposed meat. I place them on a tray and let them sit 2 to 3 days on a dark, cool shelf, letting the enzymes do their job to beef up the cubes' chances of surviving.

Have I lost you yet? You still with me? Did I go too far with the bloody stump thing?

Anyways, you have your container of choice, drainage holes in the bottom, a layer of stone, and about four inches of a good compost-and-soil mix. Let's get the cured seed cubes and get this done, because it's time to PLANT!

Remember, potatoes grow upwards, so the most important thing is to make sure the eyes and sprouts are pointing up. Lay the cubes on the bed of soil about 6 inches apart, which will maximize the growing space in the container while allowing the potatoes room to grow. A little pressure will set them in place, but there's no need to push down on the cubes because we're going to cover them anyway. Using the same compost, soil, and straw mixture, firmly place about 4 inches on top of the seed cubes. You want to give it a good first drink, watering until you see it come out of the bottom. Make sure the container is in full sun, and you're done.

Watering can be an issue with container growing because it can dry out in a blink, and as potatoes want damp, not wet, it can be a further challenge to find and maintain that happy medium. A good soak in the morning at the beginning of growing usually is enough, but as the days get warmer, you may need a lighter soak in the afternoon. The best test is just using your finger, poking the length of your finger straight down into the soil. If it is damp, you're doing ok, but if it's feeling a bit dry, adjust your watering.

Within a couple of weeks, the plant will reach the surface, breaking through with bright green foliage. Here is where you need to be the vigilant gardener and check the growth of the plant each day. I give it 3-4 inches of growth, which will happen faster than you think, before I start to mound. "Hilling" or "mounding" is done for a couple of reasons, first and foremost is to prevent potatoes from being exposed to the sun. If the runners or potatoes are exposed to sunlight, they can produce a toxic chemical called solanine, noticeable by the green color on the skin of the potato. Absorbed in large amounts, solanine can be harmful to humans... but strangely has no effect on zombies, unless you hit them on the head with the spud.

Secondly, and another debatable topic, runners that the potatoes grow on develop on the stem just under the soil surface, and by mounding, you allow for more runners to develop-- and more runners means more potatoes. I try to keep no more than an inch of the plant exposed, mounding as it grows until it reaches the rim of the container. Once you're at the rim, there is nothing else to do than to let the natural process continue, and hope the potatoes are growing and maturing underneath. Because I mound with the same compost, soil, and straw mixture, I see no need to feed the plants during the growth period, but keep a close eye on the water levels, because allowing the soil to dry out at this stage, even for a short period, can damage the plants.

HARVEST TIME

As with any of the other steps in the life of a potato, when to harvest is also up for debate. Those in colder climates will begin the harvest when the plants flower, and those in warmer climates will hold out until the plants brown and fall over. Being the Zombie Gardner, I, of course, have my own method that runs up the middle.

I am of the thought that once a plant flowers, all the energy of that plant is diverted to that flower and away from the roots and tubers. With that in mind, once I see the bud of the flower I pinch it off. Yes, I know, I can hear your gasps of breath and cries of, *Are you f'ing kidding me?*, but hear me out.

First and foremost, a pretty flower does not feed my family; larger and more abundant potatoes do. I want all the energy of that plant feeding the runners and tubers to the bitter end. Second, the plant does not need to pollinate, since whatever it was going to do, it did long before flowering. The flowers will attract more insects which, in turn, could attract larger animals, so even if pinching the bud off doesn't help with a final growth spurt, I am protecting my crop from potential dangers. You may disagree, but the voices in my head tell me I'm right, so that's my story and I'm sticking with it.

I don't consider the life cycle done until I begin to see the leaves of the plant begin to brown. Once you begin to see this, the most important thing is to stop watering. You want to do this for two reasons: once the leaves brown there is no energy left in the plant, and if the soil continues to stay wet, there is nothing protecting the tubers from beginning to rot. A dry soil also helps in the harvest by not only allowing an easier time digging the spuds out, but also by allowing the skin of the potato to dry so it doesn't get damaged during the harvest.

It can take an additional week or two from the first browning of the leaves to harvest time, and shutting down watering will expedite this. What you're looking for is to have all the foliage to fall over on its own. Don't freak out if you still see a lot of green; if the weight of the stalk becomes too much for the plant to maintain, that's the sign it's potato time.

In conventional farming or raised-bed gardening, you would pull up the foliage and gently pitch-fork the ground to bring up the potatoes, hoping you don't damage many. In container gardening, you dump, pick out, and enjoy.

I spread out a tarp so I can either repurpose the soil with a scoop or two of compost and a handful of chopped hay for the next planting, or easily re-incorporate it back into the compost pile. Tip your container over onto the tarp, and as long as you allowed the dirt to dry, it should dump out easily. Then, it's a matter of rummaging around and picking out the potatoes. Another benefit of this type of harvest is you get to see and pull out the 1-2 inch baby potatoes. Because these don't store very well most people will toss them into the compost; however, they are very tasty, and can be canned for up to a year, or you can freeze them for up to three months if you still have power.

Now, you can go from dirt to pot and still have one hell of a good-tasting potato, but like a good steak, to get the best taste out of it the potato needs to rest, or cure, for a couple days. This allows the starches from the growing process, who have been bouncing around like a 7-year-old on a sugar high, to settle back down. It also allows the skins to dry and strengthen. Strong skins are the first line of defense for long-term storage.

You need to find a dark, cool place off the ground where you can lay out the potatoes in a single row. As you lay them out, pick out any that have cuts or gashes, and anything that looks bruised or shows the beginnings of rot. Any blemishes on the skin can allow for disease and rot to set in, and in the confines of storage, it can quickly spread to the rest of your harvest. You want to set these aside for eating right away, or for canning.

I like to allow the potatoes to cure for at least three days before bagging. When choosing a bag, you want it sturdy enough to keep insects out and to keep the potatoes dry, but you also want to allow the potatoes to breathe. A burlap bag is the bag of choice, and I was lucky enough to purchase a dozen for cheap money on-line before the grid went down. In the past, I've used wooden boxes with a good half-inch between the slats to keep a good airflow, but it's not so good for storage areas that may have bug or insect problems.

For canning potatoes, I use the cold pack, or raw pack, method. Basically, I don't cook the potato before I can. I've found when you cook the potato first, it becomes too soft during the pressurizing. By the time you get to use it, the potato has become a watery mush. With a cold pack, the potatoes are only partially cooked by the end of the process and still maintain a firm shape.

Baby potatoes up to about 1 1/2 inches I keep whole; any larger, I just cut in half. For any of the damaged potatoes that I won't use right away, I cut out the damaged section and cube the rest to about inch-sized pieces. I fill these into a sterile quart-sized mason jar, up to about an inch-and-a-half below the neck of the jar, add a teaspoon of coarse salt, and fill with hot water up to an inch before the lip. Using a skewer or probe, poke it down to the bottom of the jar, moving the potatoes around to release any air bubbles that may have become trapped. Trapped air and preserving are not friends, so you want to take your time with this step. I use a cloth (or paper towel for all you Preppers) dampened with vinegar to clean the lip of the jar. This not only as a final cleaning, but to also help ensure a tighter seal. Place on a hot, sterile lid and secure with a ring, and then it's off to the pressure cooker.

Because there probably are more types of pressure cookers than people out there right now, I'm not even going to try and touch on how to use one. So let's just keep it basic: every cooker has a line inside for water level, so use that, make sure the lid of the cooker is tightly secured before you turn on the heat, and use the proper pressure for the proper times. Guessing at this can at best give you the shits, and at worst you die, neither seems like too much fun to me. Our potatoes need 30 minutes at 10 pounds pressure.

Some more common sense tips: after 30 minutes, don't try and pry the lid of the pressure cooker off because if you succeed, you're going to wish you didn't. Instead, let the pressure settle down, go and do a chore for an hour, then come back. When you do lift the lid, lift it away from you so the lid blocks the rush of steam from giving you a facial from Hell, and carefully lift out the scalding jars and place them where they can cool-- untouched-- for 24 hours. As they cool, it will create a vacuum that will seal the lid with a pop. After they have cooled, if the center of the lid can still be pressed down, you don't have a good seal, switch out the lid, and re-pressurize.

These potatoes will be good for over a year, and are perfect for home-fries, hash, or soups and stews.

By using these simple steps, you can enjoy fresh-tasting potatoes all winter long. Plant a fall crop, and you could be blessed with spuds until the spring crop is ready to harvest. Just remember to set aside a couple of the best-looking for your seed potatoes. This will ensure the good traits are passed down to future harvests.

SIMPLE POTATO HASH

I've cooked this simple, but tasty potato hash at the edge of a campfire, on a grill, or baked in a wood-fired stove. The ingredients are just as versatile, and with the base of potato, onion, garlic, and seasoning, you can add pretty much what's on hand for protein, or serve it as is. I've made this for breakfast by using leftover venison sausage, a freshly-snared rabbit, or as a side dish with just onion and some sliced green pepper. This is also the perfect recipe for those baby potatoes I told you not to throw away.

What you'll need:

1 Medium yellow onion, diced small

2 medium sized potatoes, cubed to ½ inch or smaller (or a quart of the canned potatoes)

2 garlic cloves, finely diced

Choice of meat, diced small

Available seasoning

Oil a large skillet, or if you're lucky enough to have tinfoil, oil a couple of foot-long sheets. Combine the potato, onion and garlic. For those of you who have prepped or scavenged correctly, season with salt, pepper, a teaspoon of paprika, and a teaspoon of an Italian seasoning blend. I make my own blend using herbs I've grown and dried, mixing equal amounts of basil, rosemary, thyme, oregano, and sage.

If you're using uncooked meat, simply dice up to the same size as the potato, season with salt and pepper, and add to the mixture. If you're using cooked meat, dice the same, but seasoning is not needed (unless you felt it was under-seasoned when you first had it), and add only at the last five minutes of cooking. You're just looking to heat it back up, not overcook it.

If you're using tinfoil, place the mixture in the center of the oiled sheet, then fold up the sides and crimp it, sealing the bag. Place the bag just outside the fire, but next to any glowing coals. Turn the bag every 5 minutes for about 20 minutes, or until potatoes are cooked through. You may not get the crust on the potato using this method, but it doesn't take anything away from the taste.

If you're using a stove, preheat to 350°, cook covered for 10 minutes In a skillet, then remove the cover and cook another ten minutes to get a good crust on the potato. Stir the mixture twice during the last 10 minutes.

To grill, you will need to keep the mixture moving so it doesn't burn, while also letting the potato sit long enough to build up a crust. The key is to not mash the potato in the process. Any good hash needs chunks-- not puree-- of potato. Again, it should cook a good 20 minutes or until the potato is fork-tender.

POTATO SOUP

On a cold, windy night when the meat stocks are low, or you just want something different, this is the soup to make. It's creamy, filling, and pretty damn tasty. I have a bacon source, which is why I listed it here, but any smoked or cured animal fat will do since what you're looking for is the meat flavor rendered from the fat. Also, remember that powdered milk that the apocalypse couldn't even make taste good? This is the perfect recipe for that.

What you'll need:

Strips of bacon or any smoked animal fat

1 Medium onion, diced

3 large carrots, cubed

3 stalks of celery, cubed

2 cloves garlic, minced

1 small hot pepper, finely diced for spice

6 small-to-medium potatoes, cubed

8 cups of clear broth or stock (chicken, turkey, rabbit, or vegetable)

3 tablespoon flour or thickening agent

1 cup milk

Salt and pepper to taste

Chunk up bacon and cook in a deep stew pot until bacon is crisp and all fat is rendered, and remove the bacon for later. Leave 2 to 3 tablespoons of the fat in the pot, then add onion, celery, and carrot, and sauté over medium heat until the onions begin to wilt. Add potatoes, pepper, and garlic, and let them mingle a minute or two to begin cooking and exchange flavors. Add the broth and let it slowly come to a boil, then bring it down to a simmer for 10 minutes.

Once the potato begins to soften, strain a ladle full of the vegetables out and place them into a separate bowl. Mash the vegetables as smooth as you can; it's ok if it's slightly chunky. Add back to the soup to help thicken, and continue to let simmer until the vegetables are soft. Just before serving, add the cup of powdered milk mixed with the flour if you have it. Stir it for 2 minutes and serve. You can top off the bowls with the crumbled bacon.

This dish always makes me think of cheese, remember cheese? How good this would be with some sharp cheddar sprinkled on top? Cheese, cheese, my kingdom for some cheese!

POTATO YEAST STARTER

If I were to list the number of ways I know to make bread, I wouldn't have time to write anything else, and this subject should go into another chapter. This is about potatoes, and what do potatoes have to do with bread? Well, there is potato bread of course, but more importantly, the potato can supply one of the important ingredients: yeast.

It's a bit unnerving to think about, but yeast is everywhere, and the more you bake, the more yeast will be in the air. To capture it for use in bread, beer, or alcohol, you just need a food source. Using potatoes is one of a number of ways to do this; in fact, back in the day this was used for making vodka.

Yes, before you ask: each type of yeast will slightly affect the taste of your bread. The only advice I can give you is the world has gone to shit, there is no more artisan-crafted organic overpriced loaves you can get at the store, so just get over yourself.

What you'll need:

2 cups of water

2 large unpeeled potatoes, rough chopped

2 tbsp sugar

Flour

Boil potatoes in unsalted water until soft. Strain, but save the water. In a glass bowl, mash the potatoes and add the sugar, the potato water, and enough flour to make a stiff batter. Cover with cheesecloth and place in a dark, warm place. Within a day you will see bubbles form on the batter; these are the beginnings of fermenting, and should last a day or two.

When the bubbles stop, place the mixture in a jar with a loose-fitting lid, because the dough will continue to release gasses and if not expelled, the jar could explode under the pressure-- leaving you one hell of a mess to clean up. If you still have refrigeration, the dough will last up to five days, otherwise it needs to be used within a couple of days.

Where you live, what time of year it is, and a thousand other factors can affect how much of the yeast starter you will need. In general, I substitute a cup of the yeast starter for a cup of the flour in the recipe.

SIMPLE POTATO PANCAKE

I know some of you preppers out there have stored away boxes of powered eggs thinking it would be as good as the real thing, you are wrong. I can't think of one recipe powered eggs would be good in, and this recipe is no different. The yoke provides a binding element so you have pancakes and not hash, and the yoke just tastes better. If you don't have an egg source, I suggest you find one, or barter for some chicks and have a ready source for yourself.

Another key thing in this dish is to be patient and let them cook: drop some in the skillet and let them cook, turn them over and let them cook. The more you move them around in the pan, the more chance you'll have of breaking them apart. Letting them get good and brown on each side not only enhances the flavor, but helps bind them together.

What you'll need:

2 pounds potatoes

1 small onion

1 egg

1 Tablespoon flour

Salt and pepper to taste

The trickiest part is finely grating the potato and onion. I have one of those square tin graters with different sized grates on each size. Does a real good job, but it's a bitch to clean afterwards. I use the medium size on the potatoes because I like the texture and boast of potato flavor, but the onions I grate as finely as possible. I place both the grated potato and onion in a cheese cloth and try and squeeze out as much of the juice as I can, otherwise the pancakes will be watery and turn into a potato gruel during cooking. Save the juice-- it works wonders in soups, stews, and I use it in vegetable stock.

Add egg, flour, and salt and pepper. Mix until fully combined, although it doesn't hurt the final outcome either way. I use my hands to mix to try and not break up the potato, but again, that's just a textural thing.

A well-oiled cast-iron skillet over medium heat works best for me, and if you're able to add a couple of tablespoons of bacon grease, all the better. Drop in a scoop of the mixture-- I use an old ice-cream scoop, but a ¼ cup measuring cup will work too-- and press down to flatten it out. Now, leave it alone and let it do its thing. Don't move it, don't shake the pan, don't breathe on it. Depending on how many cakes you're cooking at one time, you will need 3 to 5 minutes per side, and you will see the edges brown up when it's time to flip.

These are a good side dish for breakfast, lunch, or dinner, but now that you will listen to me and have a ready egg source, place two to three pancakes on a plate and top them with an over-easy egg. A taste of heaven, my friends, a taste of heaven.

ODDS AND ENDS

I figure most of you still remember television. It was almost ironic that just before it all went to shit, there was a reality show about Preppers. For the most part, it was silly, a number of half-hours I will never get back. One episode that really sticks out had a guy in full hazmat gear trying to make it down the busy streets of a major city to his storage rental where he kept all his stockpiles of food and water. I often wonder about that guy... I wonder if he and his family made it, or if it was a grand waste of time.

Anyway, as comical as the show got, it also offered some valuable advice on prepping. It made me aware that there are major limits to stockpiling food, far beyond the expiration dates. The main issues that revealed themselves early on was the amount of space that would be needed, the time to gather it all, and the exorbitant expense. It was clear that to have any sustainable living along with fresh and healthy food, I would need to grow, hunt, and gather it myself.

Of the items I stored are things I thought would be too hard to grow at my amateur level, would need too much space or different climate, or the process to develop was far beyond what my lazy ass wanted to do. These include flour, sugar, rice, and assorted dry beans. I divided them into vacuum bags and stored them in those five-gallon plastic buckets with oxygen absorbers. I also stored pure honey because they have an almost forever shelf-life, and it's a healthier sweetener, a perfect bartering item, and, quite frankly, bees kind of scare me.

A luxury item I stored was green coffee beans. Before the internet crashed, you could buy them in 25-pound bags, and as long as you don't roast them ahead of time they can hold up pretty well. I divided them by what I thought would be a weekly portion, sealed them in vacuum bags, and stored them in the same five-gallon buckets. When needed, I take out a bag and roast them for 20 minutes or so on the wood stove or outdoor grill. You want them to be dark brown, but not burnt. I grind them up in a hand-grinder I picked up at a flea market before the shit went down, and brew it up in an old percolator or French press. The unused portion I store in a sealed jar, and it will stay fresh for a couple of weeks.

I have no definitive comment on the shelf-life of the unroasted bean. I drink enough of it that I can't really tell a difference. I'm good for at least 2 or 3 cups a day, whereas I have a daughter that might drink 2 cups a year, but she's just not normal. She has told me she has noticed the coffee seems to get weaker with each year, but by roasting it myself, the flavor is still there so I'm OK with that.

I tell you, there is nothing better after the world has gone to shit than watching the sun rise over a deserted landscape with a hot cup of fresh coffee.

CARROTS

"Do carrots really help you see better?'"

"Well, have you ever seen a rabbit with glasses?" he replied in his best Groucho Marx impression.

Some useless information cluttering up my brain is a story that eating large quantities of carrots can cause you to see in the dark. This story comes from World War II, when British pilots became known for being able to shoot down German planes at night. The military issued a story that this was because of the high amounts of carrots the pilots were eating, giving them superhuman night vision. In reality, this was a story drummed up to keep the Germans from discovering the British had a new invention they were using called "radar."

But there is some truth to the old wives' tales. Carrots have loads of beta-Carotene, which the body changes into vitamin A. The retina needs vitamin A for good eye health, and especially for night vision. Carrots also have vitamins C, B1, B2, B6 fiber, potassium, thiamine, calcium, and iron. One cup contains about 70 calories, can reduce cholesterol levels, and is packed full of energy. *Eat three carrots and you'll have enough energy to walk three miles*, an old saying goes. It's like Mother Nature's One-A-Day. But you have to cook it to get the best of it.

Carrots are one of the few vegetables that are actually better for you cooked. I won't bore you with the science, but the body cannot break down raw carrot enough to get at all the good stuff. The cooking process helps break down the cell walls that hold in all the nutrients, allowing the body to absorb them better. This still doesn't mean to cook the damn things to death; I like mine with a bit of bite left in them.

Although not hard, growing carrots can have its challenges. Seeding can take up to two growing seasons, and the seeds are so small they can be difficult to handle. You need deep, loose, and sandy soil, and over-fertilizing can change a sleek, sweet-tasting carrot into a gnarled, woody piece of crap. The payoff is if you get it right, carrots are a healthy, sustainable food source that stores well, has a long shelf-life, and pretty much can go with any meal.

Some more useless carrot information:

Mirepoix is the French foundation for most sauces and broths which includes carrots, onion, and celery. Yes, it is true that if you eat too large a quantity of carrots, your skin can turn orange. This happens only on the palms and soles of your feet and is completely harmless. To correct it, just cut down on the carrots. When storing carrots, if they seem a little soft and limp (sorry men, no other way to say it), toss the carrots into some cold water for a few minutes and they will firm and crisp right up. Carrot seeds are so small that a teaspoon can hold over 2000 of them.

I'll end this with an old Irish proverb:

Never bolt your door with a boiled carrot.

SEEDING

Carrots are second only to beets in sweetness, but this is because of nature's grand design. They are biennial, meaning the first year the plant uses its energy to grow the tap root, which we mistakenly call the carrot, and this is where it stores all its sugars. In the second year, it releases these sugars to produce the flowers and seeds. It's as simple as that.

Well, there may be a couple more steps you need to take.

First of all, I will make a giant assumption here: I will assume you either came across a package of carrot seeds, and by sheer dumb luck managed to grow a couple, or stumbled upon a carrot bed in its first year of growth, or bartered some carrots and had the sense to try and regrow one. I know, pretty bold of me, but we've gotta start somewhere.

As with most crops you want to seed, you should pick out the best of that crop in the hopes that the future crops will carry all the good attributes forward. Only, unlike other crops, you need to first harvest carrots to find the ones you want to seed. A bit unnerving, I agree, but not as difficult as it first seems. Carrots are a hardy crop and once you choose which ones you're seeding, just put them back in the ground to finish out the season.

If you're in the warmer climates, you can cover them with a good layer of mulch or straw and just leave them in the ground all winter. There will be some slow growth, but I'll bet my crossbow that allowing the carrot to slow-grow through the winter will produce seeds that will give you a hardier crop next season. Here in the Northeast, there are a few more steps I need to take.

My main goal is to keep the seed carrot in the ground for as long as possible, but to harvest it before the first frost. I know, I know, I get it, no more weather reports so how can you tell when a frost is coming? One way is by the late-day temperatures. If you feel a sudden drop in the late afternoon, it's a safe bet the drop will continue into the night, and then you can do the math to see if it will reach frost temperatures. You'll be right only half the time, but your seed carrots will be safe all the time. Then again, you can let the carrot tell you when it's ready. When the foliage begins to yellow and droop over, pick them.

Unlike harvesting for food, which we will get to in a moment, when I harvest seed carrots, I leave the foliage on. Storing these carrots are also a shade different: I 'replant' them in a bucket of damp sand. I'm looking to stunt the growth for the winter, and the sand will limit nutrients to the carrot which will naturally hibernate until you replant it in a dirt bed.

I keep the sand bucket with the seed carrots in the same dark, cool place I keep my other root vegetables. Only the seed carrots go to the coldest section as cold, not freezing, helps the carrot mature. The carrot needs to be in the mature stage to seed, which happens in cold or cooler weather, which is why if you're in warm climates and can allow the plant to winterize in the ground, you'll get a stronger seed.

I stress keeping the sand damp, not wet. You do not want the carrot to dry out because it will die and not go to seed the next season, but you also do not want the sand too wet or the carrot will rot and there will be nothing left to go to seed. During your normal maintenance of your food storage, stick your finger in the sand; if it feels dry, take a spray bottle and give it a few good squirts of water.

As the daytime temperature gets just above freezing, I place the buckets of seed carrots outside to acclimate. I give it a couple of days of getting used to the outside temperatures before replanting. I plant in the same loose, deep soil, but I try and keep it away from whatever bed I plan to use for a regular harvest. Maybe it's just my paranoia taking over, but I don't want the seed carrots taking anything away from this year's harvest, and I don't want this year's harvest taking anything away from the carrots I want to go to seed. I know, a better man would have just said to avoid cross-pollination. But, what's the fun in that?

Within 6 to 8 weeks, you will see a thick stem shoot up from the carrot. The stem will develop an umbrella-shaped foliage at the top of it, which will begin to sprout out tiny white flowers. This is the seed head, but you need to let the flowers do their thing, so just let it be. Once the flowers die out then you can cut the seed heads off, leaving just enough of the stem to grab onto, and put each one in its own brown paper bag to store in a cool, dark place to dry.

Chances are you will be up to your eyebrows in harvests of other crops to keep your mind off the seed heads, which is good because you need to let them fully dry. Let's face it: you don't need them until at least the following season. It's the perfect time to take care of the long list of crap that needs to be done before the fall season sets in and distracts you, so the seed heads can do what seed heads do.

On a crisp, fall day with nothing on your To-Do List, take one of the bags and grab onto the stem of the dried seed head. While still in the bag, shake the shit out of it, banging the head against the insides of the bag. When there is nothing left to fall out, toss the seed head in the compost pile. At the bottom of the bag you'll have a little chaff and a lot of seed; in fact, each head will give you a couple of few thousand seeds.

I wouldn't worry too much about the chaff, but if you're looking for a cleaner storage, the best way I've found is using the wind. Find a breezy spot and lay down any type of white cloth or paper. Keeping your hands about three feet above the ground, firmly rub the seeds between your hands. This will break up the chaff, allowing the wind to carry it away while the heavier seeds fall to the cloth. This method also crumbles away the fuzzy coating that surrounds the seed. I've never found the coating to be an issue if left on, but if it betters your chances at a harvest, then why not remove it?

I don't like handling seeds too much so I'll repeat this process two, maybe three times. If the chaff is heavy and you plant some of the chaff with the seed, it really is not a problem. Carrot seeds can be planted right away without any drying, and you can store them for up to three years. I keep all seeds in envelopes I've collected, because what else am I going to do with them? Who the hell am I going to write to, and how the hell am I going to mail it? I mark the envelope with type and date and store them away from sunlight.

I created a seed box. I took an old wooden tool box with two levels, keeping herbs on the top and vegetables and fruits on the bottom. Each level is separated by germination times so when March hits, I easily know which seeds to start with by grabbing the envelopes from that section, and so on with April, May, and into the next fall. Trust me, I'm normally not that organized, but it is a cool system.

PRE-PLANTING

When getting ready for planting carrots you need only a couple of things: first and foremost you need loose, sandy soil; you need it to be at least 12 inches deep (a bonus to have it 6 or more inches above the ground); and you need a thick skin when the seedlings sprout.

You would think that deep, loose soil 6 inches or more above ground is the perfect candidate for containers, and it is, but hear me out and listen to the flaw in this theory. Unlike potatoes, in which one plant can produce a half-dozen spuds or more, the carrot produces only one. The amount of containers you would need to get enough of a harvest to last the winter, especially with limited garden space, will quickly chip away the ability to plant other crops. The math just doesn't add up.

A five-gallon container will safely give you 6 to 8 carrots, while a 10-foot by 4-foot raised bed will give you four rows of 20 to 25 carrots. That will give you a harvest of as many as 100 carrots. To get 100 carrots from containers, you would need as many as 17. Try and visualize what 17 containers would look like, and then how much soil you will need to fill them. I still use containers to round out the harvest, but I find it makes more sense in a raised bed. Besides, just because you're living in the apocalypse doesn't mean you have to live like *Mad Max*-- a working garden can still look nice.

The reasoning behind using a raised bed of 6 inches or more is because of the carrot fly. This pesky insect can wage the perfect storm on your crop by laying its eggs near the carrot, and when the larvae hatch, they will attack the foliage and eat their way through the root-- leaving you with a carrot with holes tunneled through it. To make matters worse, some of the carrot flies' eggs can take a year to hatch, so if you don't rotate your crop next year, the larvae will attack the seeds and seedlings.

Mother Nature has supplied us with some tricks to battle the fly, specifically with the height of your planting. Carrot flies are low-flying insects, and I've read they fly as low as 3 inches to a high of 20 inches above ground. Now, I hear you, having a 20-inch high raised bed can be impractical, but there are ways around that. Back when the world was normal, an old neighbor of mine used a white landscaping cloth to build a 3-foot-high barrier to box around his carrot crop. Some of the larger farms would lay this cloth over the seedlings, when they were more apt to attract the fly.

I know some of these specialty items are hard to come by these days, but any white cloth that is thin enough to allow light and water through will do the trick. You don't have to be fancy, just keep it between 2 and 3 feet high, and build it around the bed. The flies do not have the ability to fly over this so you don't need to close the top off, and as long as water and light get through, you can leave it up until harvest.

Another of Mother Nature's tricks involves simple camouflage. The main attraction for the fly is the scent the carrot produces when leaves are bruised or torn. This happens mostly during thinning of the seedlings, and is unavoidable. I address this in two ways: I water the bed immediately after thinning to help keep the scent down, and I plant a border of onions or garlic around the bed. This not only helps mask the scent of the carrot, but they keep away any small rodents that might want to use your carrot bed as their own personal grocery store.

PLANTING

Carrot seeds are small, we can all agree on that. It's because of the small size that you're going to plant more seeds then you will need to. Because seeds can be in high demand, and carrot seeds are harder to come by, you're going to have to grow some tougher skin and realize the planting process will produce some waste. Just deal with it.

Carrots need 60 to 75 days from seed to harvest, so, like potatoes, ideally you can get a summer and a fall crop if you time the seedlings right. Just remember: one of the best defenses against the carrot fly is to rotate where you plant each harvest, and make sure the soil has been turned and aged well before planting the seeds. Fresh compost can not only burn the seeds before they germinate, but it can harm the carrots' growth pattern, causing unsightly and inedible appendages to grow out and sap the carrot of all that is good.

Because carrots don't like to be transplanted, preferring to germinate directly in the soil, you need to sow your first crop soon after the threat of a frost. Carrot seeds behave best when the soil is around 60° within the top two inches of soil, and before you start whining about no thermometers, just put your big panties on and grab a handful of soil and work it between your hands. The soil will always tell you by look, by feel, and by smell if it's happy or not.

I use an old yardstick that I rub back and forth in the soil until I have at least a half-inch deep groove, keeping the rows 6-8 inches apart because it's just easier to maintain weed control with that spacing. Now, I've tried everything I could think of to conserve seed use. One harvest, I even started by using a tweezer to individually plant each seed. After just half a row, I figured it would take me until fall to get the spring crop in, and that killed that idea. The best method I've come up with is fingertips and a pinch.

I pour no more than half a teaspoon in the palm of one hand, and take a small pinch using the thumb and forefinger of my other hand. Over the rows you just made, rub your thumb and forefinger together allowing the seeds to fall into the groove as evenly-spaced as you can. Once you've finished with the row, use the same thumb and forefinger on each side of the trench to pinch the soil closed. All that's left is a good mist of water for the seeds, and a good drink of homemade wine for you.

Be patient: carrot seeds can take 14 to over 20 days to begin germination, depending on soil conditions and temperatures. You do want to keep the soil damp so a top crust doesn't get established which prevents the seedlings from breaking ground. Birds do find carrot seedlings mighty tasty, so as the green stems break ground if you have a bird cloth or anything that will allow sun and water through but keep birds out, this is the time to use it. Once the seedlings reach 3-4 inches tall, it is time to put your big panties back on and thin the herd.

There are two methods of thinning: you can either cut the stems you want to thin out at ground level, or pull out the seedlings. To be honest, I use both. I will use an old moustache trimmer I've acquired along the way and cut out the seedlings closest to the ones I want to keep, then pull out everything else in between. What I'm left with is rows of seedlings that are around 3 inches apart, giving the carrots space to grow as long and fat as the garden fairies will allow.

As I pointed out above, this is the time to give a good watering and put up your protective netting because the microscopic oil produced by thinning may not smell like anything to you, but it's like ringing a dinner bell for the Carrot Fly.

You want to keep the carrots well-watered and weeded. You also want to look out for that stray plant that thinks it's in its second year of life. I've never been able to discover why, but in some cases a carrot will go to seed soon after germinating-- not often, but every two to three harvest you can get one. You will see a thick stalk growing up in between the normal foliage, and if you're quick enough and cut the stalk away before it drains energy from the root, you can save the carrot; however, in most cases I've found that the carrot turns woody and tasteless. I also have never allowed the head to go to early seed. Think about that for a moment: something broke inside the carrot factory, allowing this plant to seed early, so why would I want to carry on that trait and grow generations of a broken carrot?

NOTE: Throughout this section, I have stressed that carrots like to be sowed directly into the soil, as the fragile seedlings can't handle the shock of transplanting. This is a rule I urge all of you to follow for your main planting. With that said, I have discovered you can fool the seedlings and add to your harvest.

For most of you, ice cubes are a thing of the past, and with no power, the one place you avoid when scavenging an abandoned house is the refrigerator-- and for good reason. But early in the destruction, I came upon an open stand-up freezer that was totally cleaned out except for a dozen ice cube trays. I have no idea why I took them, other than they were different bright colors: purple, red, blue and pink. They were also smaller than the usual trays by half.

About two years later, I came upon them in a box in the shed, only most were now cracked and pretty useless for anything. I thought that at the very least they could be used as seed starters, and that thought soon evolved to carrots and my lack of being able to extend my limited growing season. I cut out the bottoms and laid the trays on a screened drying rack, filled them with soil, and planted the carrot seeds. There still is some thinning, but for the most part, once the seedling is about 3 inches tall you can replant.

I use this method for containers, as a way to bridge between the harvests. I gently push the soil up from the bottom of the tray so I have a solid cube. Using the same soil in the container, I transplant the carrot, taking as much care to keep the cube together in the hopes the seedling doesn't feel the shock of the transplant. This works about 60 percent of the time.

HARVESTING

You can begin to harvest carrots before they fully mature after around 50 days. It's what the old world used to call baby carrots. They're not as sweet, but they are tender and quite tasty. I've been known to sneak one or two for a quick pick-me-up when working in the garden. The container crops are perfect for baby carrots, but I wouldn't want to use your main crops for this. The goal is to harvest enough to get you through the winter.

For spring harvest, I use two methods to determine if the carrots have matured. The best method is the calendar, or however you mark off the days now. Carrots need at least two and a half months to mature-- a good 70 days or more is the rule of thumb-- and some gardeners look for a ½ to ¾ inch thickness at the top. In general, I follow this rule, but I also use a second method that has not failed me yet.

I'm not sure of the science as to why, but as a carrot reaches maturity, it will begin to push itself up out of the ground. We're not talking waking up one morning and finding carrots magically out of the ground ready for you to pick up; what you are looking for is around a half-inch of the top poking up above the soil, and with the spring crop you don't want to let it go too long because the heat of the summer will make carrots get woody and . . . well, they taste like shit.

I have found, unlike potatoes, if I water just before I harvest the carrots, it helps loosen the soil so the root comes up pretty easily. Just grab where the stalk meets the root and gently pull up, twisting a little as the soil gives up its grip. If you feel any resistance, then stop and loosen the soil around the carrot with a garden trowel. You do not want to snap the carrot in half.

Fall crops have the added question of demographics thrown into the mix. As long as the outside temperature stays above freezing, you can keep the carrot in the ground and pick as you need. As the temp falls below 60°, the root stops growing, and the ground becomes the perfect root cellar. For added protection, lay down a good 6 inches or more covering of mulch to protect against an unexpected frost.

In my neck of the woods, I will harvest the rest of the crop before the first frost and store for winter use. In areas of milder winters, you can keep them in the ground right up until spring. I would still suggest a thick layer of mulch, and you will need to harvest everything but your seed carrots by spring when the temps begin to rise. You need to remember that below 60°, carrots will stop growing and maintain a good texture and taste, above 60° and the carrot will continue to grow to a point where it is nothing more than a tree branch.

No matter the method of harvest, at some point you will need to think about long-term storage. Carrots, like most root crops, store well with just a little preparation. A box, some wood chips, and a spray bottle, and you can have carrots in February during a raging blizzard that taste like they were just picked from the ground.

The two most important things you need for good storage is below 60° and dampness. The first thing I do when I harvest carrots is to chop off the head to remove the foliage. This will not only stunt the carrot from any more growth, but it will also prevent the leaves from taking any sweetness away from the root. Any carrots that are deformed, bruised, or otherwise damaged I'll set aside for canning, because all you need is one carrot going bad to ruin all the rest.

I use a wooden box that over the years has developed spaces between the slats; this allows for some airflow. You can use any type of container as long as you make a couple holes in it-- the air helps keeps the chips from becoming over-damp and causing rot.

I put down a layer of wood chips that are soaked overnight in water, then lay down a row of carrots making sure they don't touch each other, which helps stop the spread of rot if one carrot does go bad. I repeat this until either the box is full, or I run out of carrots. I store the box in the cellar and keep a spray bottle filled with water next to it. During my normal winter chores, I will give the wood chips a good spray, or when anyone takes carrots out, they give it a squirt. What you're looking for is to keep the chips damp, not wet, and don't let them dry out.

What you're trying to do here is trick the carrots into thinking they are still alive, in the ground and hibernating. I've had success with this method for over three months, where the last carrot out of the box tasted almost as fresh as the first.

I raw-pack the odd or damaged carrots for canning, meaning I don't precook before putting into the pressure canner. I like to cut them in slices ¼ inch or larger so they don't get mushy during the process. I tightly pack the slices into hot sanitized jars, leaving a good inch of headspace. Toss in ½ teaspoon of salt and fill up to the inch of headspace with boiling water, wipe rim, place on a sanitized lid, and tighten down with a jar band. I process at 15 pounds for 30 minutes.

Let these sit to cool overnight before storing away from heat and sun. They will keep well in sealed jars for over a year, but in my homestead, the jars never make it to spring.

CANNING GLAZED CARROTS

In the middle of winter, vegetables you canned yourself are the next thing to fresh in my book. But, let's be truthful here for a moment: when you're stuck inside for a couple of days because a storm's raging outside, both food and time can get a touch boring. I can't do much about keeping your mind from going bat-shit crazy, but I do have a few recipes that help keep the dinner table interesting, and this is the canning recipe I save for just those days-- helps zing things up a bit.

What you'll need:

Enough sliced, uncooked carrots to fill 4 pint canning jars

2 cups brown sugar (If you haven't prepped or scavenged brown sugar, then use a teaspoon at a time of molasses added to a cup of sugar until you get the same effect. Just add brown sugar and molasses to your scavenger list.)

2 cups of water

1 cup of orange juice (I've tried apple juice which is more available to me, and it's good, but not the same. Every chance to trade for oranges I take, and at least 1 cup of the juice is saved for this recipe.)

Make sure the carrot-filled jars have at least a 1-inch headspace. Mix the rest of the ingredients into a pot and heat until fully melted. Pour contents over the jarred carrots, again leaving a 1-inch headspace. Because of the grit from un-melted sugar, or pulp from the orange juice, you need to take extra care in cleaning the rims of the jar. Seal the jars with a sanitized lid and jar band, and place in your canner.

I process these at 15 pounds for 30 minutes and then allow to cool overnight before storing them away from heat and sun. You should get at least a year's shelf-life, but to be honest, they are so good that I have never been able to keep a jar past one winter.

Serving them is just as easy. The canning process will cook the carrots halfway or more, depending on the size of the slices, and the flavor from the glaze is throughout. I just pour them, glaze and all, into a saucepan and heat and serve. There was one time I got distracted and allowed the glazed carrots to overcook, so I mashed them with a pinch of cinnamon and it was heaven on a plate. The next morning, I mixed in a raw egg, and diced onion and potatoes, and made a hash out of it. Survival at its best.

STEWED CABBAGE AND CARROTS

Before the collapse, I could point to one thing I could honestly say I didn't like: cabbage. I could handle it raw, but I didn't like the smell of it cooking or the texture of it after it was cooked, but things do change. When a zombie-infected population turns society upside down, you begin to rethink your likes and dislikes, and cabbage moved onto my OK list. Because cabbage works well with carrots, this quickly became a favorite of mine. We make it during the fall not only because that is when the cabbage crop is ready, but also because the weather still allows for the windows to stay open. Cabbage not only smells while cooking during the day, but it also makes you fart during the night.

What you'll need:

1 large head of cabbage, green works best but red will do

4 to 6 slices bacon- Get a bacon source!

1 cup water

3 to 4 large carrots, sliced

1 hot pepper of your choice, diced

1 stalk of celery, diced

3 cloves garlic, smashed

In a large, deep pan you want to render the fat out of the bacon on low heat. I slow cook this until the bacon can be crumbled, and put the bacon aside. Bringing the heat up to medium, I add the cabbage to cook it down so everything else will fit. Add the rest of the ingredients except the crumbled bacon, and simmer for at least two hours until the carrots are tender. Serve hot with the crumbled bacon sprinkled on top.

SIMPLE CARROT SOUP

The best thing about this recipe is that you can get away with using mostly scraps for the main ingredient. We will make a big batch of this during the carrot harvest and canning season. Most of the cut ends, peelings, and just about anything too good for the compost bin can be used for this soup. We then put it into quart canning jars, minus the milk, and process it the same as the whole carrots. When needed, you empty a jar in a pot, add milk, and heat. Serve this for lunch on a brisk afternoon with a grilled sandwich and there is nothing better than that.

What you'll need:

2 pounds carrots, diced

1 medium onion, diced

4 cups whatever broth you have on hand, chicken and vegetable work best

1 tablespoon of grated ginger (A future book will show growing ginger, not as hard as you may think.)

Salt and pepper to taste

½ cup of milk (The powdered stuff works well here, as does goat milk.)

In a large pot, "sweat" the onions. This is a process that with a little oil and low heat, you cook the onions until they are translucent, but don't let them brown. Add the carrots, broth, and ginger, and simmer on medium heat until the carrots easily break apart at the touch.

If you have power and a blender, you'll want to blend this until smooth. Just remember: hot liquid will expand when agitated, so do this in small batches. For the rest of the backwoods world, you can use a simple potato masher. Drain and save the liquid, and mash the carrot and onion as you slowly add the liquid back in. I have a ricer, which, for lack of a better description, is a garlic press on steroids, and I rice up the solids then whisk back in the liquid. It comes out surprisingly smooth for a little bit of effort.

If you're serving this right away, add your milk and reheat until hot. Add salt and pepper to taste and enjoy.

Note: Because some of the old world still rears its ugly head now and then, I feel compelled to make this public service announcement: if you are using powdered milk, please, please, please mix the milk as directed on the package first, then add the liquid milk to the soup mixture. Please do not add a half cup of powder to the soup. Thank you. We will now resume to your regular scheduled program.

PICKLED CARROTS

I understand many people will not have some of these ingredients, but most of these can be easily made or grown, and at the very least should be added to your list of things to look for when out scavenging.

Here's the thing about pickled vegetables-- I think they are a fun and versatile way of having vegetables on hand at any given time. Think about it: after a long, hot day on the homestead, you don't feel like cooking a meal so you toss some smoked meat between two pieces of bread and fill a bowl with some pickled vegetables. Add a mug of home brew, a rocker, and your front deck, and that's a damn fine way to end the day.

We also, despite the fact we try hard to stay secluded, welcome visits from surviving family and friends from time to time. Pickled vegetables are the perfect entertaining food for when you're catching up on the news of our small world, or haggling over bartering. They are simple, tasty, and adds a bit of flavor to an otherwise simple life. Just because we have been thrown back hundreds of years doesn't mean we're dead.

What you'll need:

1 pound of carrots, sliced (I cut them into 3-4 inch sticks just because it's a little different, but cutting them into coin shapes works just as well.)

1 cup of apple cider (This is not that difficult to make, and in another book I will touch on that.)

¼ cup sugar

2 tablespoons of salt

1 tablespoon of black peppercorns

1 tablespoon of mustard seed

The process is fairly simple. Place all the ingredients, except the carrots, into a pot and bring to a boil. Place the carrots into a sterilized canning jar and pour the liquid in, leaving an inch of headspace. Seal with a sterilized lid and jar band, and place into a hot water bath for 10 minutes, making sure the water is at least an inch over the top of the jars. Let the jars cool overnight and store in a dark, cool place.

Because of the high acid levels, most pickling does not need pressurized canning, and can get by with a simple hot water bath. A hot water bath is submerging the sealed canning jars into rapidly boiling water for a set time.

You can enjoy these right away, but I've found that letting them sit for at least two to three weeks allows the pickling liquid to penetrate the carrot.

ODDS AND ENDS

I think it was when I began stocking up on weapons that the family began to take notice. It wasn't so much the guns and ammo-- they would have easily written that off as midlife crisis-- but the crossbow, longbow, and snares made them all begin to think not only was I serious about this, but I may be one step closer to my first pair of Depends and a trip to the nursing home.

Today, of course, they will say they were behind me all the time, and in some ways I believe they were. In truth, some days they were concerned but also somewhat relieved that I was doing what I was doing, and other days I think they were just concerned. In hindsight, it's just tough being the one person left that is right all the time.

The days of "Fun with Weapons" are long over. It's all serious business now; you use your weapons for two reasons, and two reasons only. You use them to help put food on your family's table, and, more importantly, you use them to protect your family, your home, and yourself from all predators both human and animal alike. A hungry dog can be as dangerous as a pack of humans, and vice versa.

The weapons I depend on the most I collected long before the world decided to take a large shit on the human population. To be honest, the last couple years I've found one useful .22 pistol that is not much good except for shooting the squirrels that try to invade the garden. I've found a number of rusted-out firearms that I couldn't get to fire, so I broke them down for parts. In some cases, I've been able to trade the parts for ammo or other goods.

This doesn't mean you should give up. Even though most stores were picked clean within a week after the crash, there are still some hidden gems out there. Don't just check out houses: look through garages, sheds, and check for hidden bunkers. Preppers were very good at creating hiding places. If you're brave enough, or stupid enough, areas with the highest number of infected also have the most places unexplored, and you have a better chance of finding firearms and ammo there.

I can't help you get weapons, but I can help you know what to get. We won't get into name brands because they carry no weight anymore. Sure, some name brands are better quality, but when you're facing a horde of infected, will it really matter if you have a Glock or Uncle Bob's revolver?

I feel it's important to have at least one pistol for protection, and I am never without my 9mm semi-auto. I also have the .22mm that I found, but the 9mm gives me a better sense of security. I'm not promoting 9mms here, just saying that having a larger caliber pistol on your side will give you more options for close-up protection.

I also suggest a shotgun, which can play two roles in the survival game. I have a 12-gage pump and I have to tell you that nothing gets the attention of a dangerous stranger more than the *chuck, chik* sound of pumping a round in the chamber. Again, this is an up-close and personal kind of weapon, but depending on the shot you use, you can hit more with less. It's the shotgun's role in hunting that I think is more important. A good shotgun can supplement your meat stocks with a variety of smaller game like pheasant, turkey, and duck. Surviving the apocalypse is stressful enough without being able to have a good meal or two every once in a while.

For larger game, I use a bolt action 30-06 that has a decent scope on it. With a major reduction in the human population, the deer and wild boar populations around here have exploded. There is also the problem that most people didn't think of before the crash: there was a fair amount of animals tossed into the wild when all the zoos collapsed. For the most part, these animals avoid any human contact, but they have already produced a new generation that has no fear of man. You are going to need a rifle with some kick to it.

This gun works well on the infected also. Unlike the Zombies of lore you don't need a head shot, although it doesn't hurt. They will bleed out and die just like the rest of us, they will starve like the rest of us and freeze like the rest of us. Only the virus will live in the fluids long after the host is gone, so if the body fluids enters a water source, or gets licked up by the family dog who goes home afterwards and kisses everybody, well then, . . . you got problems.

For the small game like rabbit, I always keep a .22 rifle on hand as well. I have to admit that back when the world was right, I would have told you eating squirrel would have to be one of the most disgusting things you could eat. Right up there with that bald, fat guy who became famous on a TV show where he ate bugs, insects, and goat balls. Well, time does have a way of changing everything. Today, I will tell you that when lightly seasoned, browned, and added to a pot of sliced potatoes, carrots, and onions in a vegetable broth, then simmered for three hours, well... it's so good, it is almost orgasmic. We're talking squirrel here, not goat balls. The end of the world still has limits. But, you will need a .22 rifle to get those fast bastards.

Not all is *click-click, bang-bang* in the hunting world. You will also need fishing gear, a pole or two and some basic tackle. Although I do have some deep sea equipment, I have kept mostly to fresh water. The few times I've made it back to the sea, I've stayed on shore for the shellfish. I do have a couple of Yo-Yo Traps, which are what they sound like. They are the size and shape of a yo-yo, only they hold fishing line, and you secure them on a tree branch, or side of a boat, and allow the line to drop in the water. If a fish takes the bait, the Yo-Yo Trap will automatically snap back to secure the hook and reel the fish in for you.

Once again, you no longer have the luxury of hanging your hat on just one hook. When scavenging, you need to also look for bows and arrows, crossbows, and compound bows. With some practice, you can feed your family indefinitely with one bow and one arrow.

ONION

I consider the onion one of the healthiest and most versatile foods in the apocalypse. It's fairly easy to grow, stores well, and in my opinion, is a must-have for almost any meal you cook. In all honesty, if I were to lose the ability to grow onions it would make a noticeable impact on my life, and of all the things we quickly have gotten used to not having, I would deeply notice the absence of onions.

I'm not being melodramatic here, so let me put this in the simplest way I know. Most of us woke up on that Wednesday morning a few years ago to very different lives. We took a hot shower by simply turning a knob marked with an *H*, dressed in clothes readily cleaned in the washer and dryer in the basement, and chose which of the many restaurants we were going to patronize for breakfast that morning. Some of us went to work, others celebrated the birth of a child or mourned the death of a loved one, but we all innocently made it through our days looking forward to the weekend, vacation, or the day when we could retire. We went to bed that night feeling safe and somewhat content in the life we'd created for ourselves.

When we woke up on Thursday, the world as we knew it was over. There was no shower because there was no running water, no electricity to heat the water or run the washer and dryer. Without electricity, none of the shops were open, and within a few days they were all looted and destroyed. We went from worrying about drama on social media to stressing over how to actually survive from one day to the next.

Most were not ready for anything that catastrophic, and the new emotional and physical stresses that came with the apocalypse were more than they could handle. Those of us who have survived quickly learned that securing a sustainable food source kept us physically healthy, but it was the simplest things that strengthen us emotionally, and nothing brings a sense of comfort like a good home-cooked meal, which is where the onion plays center stage.

This is only my preference, but I grow twice as many yellow as I do red. The reasoning is that red onion works better raw. They are great on salads, in relishes, or even pickled. They bring on that extra kick that the yellow onion misses. Yet, the yellow onion works best cooked because it melds better with the food it's dancing with. When raw, the yellow onion will clash, or overpower, some flavors. When cooked, it will enhance those same flavors.

When it comes to the onion, it is not all emotional; they are a rich source of vitamin c, manganese, fiber, and B-complex. Onions are known to help in insulin production, blood flow, and aid in digestion. They also, in a number of ways, aid in the relief of cold and flu symptoms.

Old folklore stated that a flu epidemic in 1919, which took the lives of an estimated 20 to 40 million people worldwide, hit an English village pretty hard. The village doctor exhausted himself trying to get to each family to offer what little comfort he could. He was shocked when he got to one farmhouse and found the family relatively healthy.

The farmer explained that when the family began to feel the onset of the flu, his wife placed an unpeeled onion in each room. Within a day the household felt better, and have not felt any illness since. The doctor, intrigued, asked if he could take the onions back to his office to examine. Placing a cut section under a microscope, he was amazed to see the slice was indeed infested with the flu virus.

Now, there is no way to prove this story one way or the other, and I can only offer my own experiences.

My wife uses a more modern approach to this, and at the first complaint of not feeling good, she will cut the ends of an onion, stick a fork in one end, and stick the fork into a mason jar. Sometimes in a matter of a 24-hour period, the onion turns black with all the bad air it has absorbed, and all of us feel better. Psychosomatic? Maybe, but it really doesn't matter if it works or it's just in my head, as long as we're feeling better.

During the Civil War, Ulysses S. Grant sent a telegram that he was not moving his troops one inch until his onion stocks were replenished. Not only did onions spice up the otherwise bland meals of the troops, but when applied to wounds, the drawing effect of the onions helped clean them. A shipment of onions was sent the next day.

SEEDING

Like carrots, onions are biennial and will go to seed in the second year. They need to go through a growth, a cold hibernation, and then a second year of growth to produce seeds. Also like carrots, each onion seed head will produce a few thousand seeds, so I always plan to have at least 4 to 5 yellow per 3 red onions go to seed. This gives me enough for the next year's crop, and as you can squeeze 2 years of storage out of them, it gives me a safety net in case we have a bad crop in any year. I also like to keep enough to share or trade.

I use the same process for yellow and red, and only use onions from the fall crop for seeding because it's easier to get them to the temps I need. Just before harvesting the fall crop, I will gently pull up the onions I want to seed and cut back the leaves to about 2-3 inches above the bulb to try and keep as much of the energy in the bulb as possible. I store them in the coldest part of the cellar, laying them out in single rows in an open box, trying to get them to a temperature of 45 to 55° for as long as possible, and force hibernation within a couple weeks.

In warmer climates, there's not much you need to do. I would suggest a good 3-4 inches of mulch to protect against any possible frost, and when the ground temp is getting back up to the 55° mark, remove the mulch and let it do its thing.

In colder areas, once early spring hits and the ground approaches that 55° mark, you will need to replant. I'm trying not to sound like a broken record here, so just follow the same procedures as you would carrots. Allow the onion to flower and when the flowers die off, cut the stalk and place the seed head in a bag to dry. Once dry, shake the shit out of it, banging the head against the bag and allowing the seeds to fall out. You can use the same hand-rub-and-wind technique to dethatch the seeds, but the thatch doesn't hurt it. Now all you need to do is place them in an envelope, label them, and add them to your seed storage.

PRE-PLANTING

Onions need time, and to have a strong late summer crop, you need to think late winter to begin seedlings. In warmer climates, you can sow seeds directly into the ground; but in colder areas, you need to prepare a couple of extra steps. You're going to need deep trays, a warm sunny spot indoors, and a way to keep the cat from snacking on the leaves.

Your next step is figuring out how many you are going to plant. I assure you, it is a harder question to answer than you may think, and if there ever comes a time I run out of onions, I just might cry. The math I use (and I really hate math), is my family consumes approximately 4 to 5 onions a week. I need to factor into these numbers that some of that consumption will be what I've already prepared, canned, and pickled. Then consider that, especially in the deep winter months, stews and soups will be the meal of the day, and a good stew can be spread out over 3 meals. With all that said, I try and get no less than 100 yellow and 20 to 30 red onions cured and stored, or stewed and pickled, by the onset of winter.

I use a 12-foot by 3-foot raised bed that will give me about 130 bulbs. Containers seem like a waste of space for onions; by using 6-8 inches of some good, loose soil close to the ground, the onions will do fine. Onions are also a good border crop, helping keep the small critters away, and works well with some crops. On average, border onions get me an additional 20 to 30 bulbs. When you take out the small and damaged that need to be used right away, this still gets me to my goal.

Just keep in mind that while the bulb is maturing, the onion will get thirsty and hungry. During the early stage, I try to water each morning as the spring temps grow warmer, trying to give the crop at the very least an inch of water a week. Broken record time: watering each morning doesn't mean over-watering, as you can rot the bulbs quicker then they will grow. A good, loose soil for drainage, and some common sense should help you, and if you've just had a heavy spring rain you will not need to water for a day or two.

I feed the crop every two weeks or so until the bulb becomes pronounced. I use a compost tea that I ladle around the plant, but not on top of it. I'm looking to feed the soil, which in turn will safely feed the plant. I have a recipe for a simple compost tea at the end of this chapter.

PLANTING

I try to sow onion seeds in late January, no later than first week of February. During my many scavenging trips I've collected a fair amount of deep plastic seeding flats, but most trays will work for this. I suggest they be at least 4-6 inches deep and have some drainage to avoid drowning the seeds before they can germinate.

I use a good composted soil that I allowed to get to room temperature, and sow the seeds at ¼ inch deep. I use a spray bottle to wet the soil down, which helps give the seeds a good drink without flooding them. The seeding flats I have came with a plastic cover which helps keep the humidity in, but placing twigs 8-10 inches long in each corner and in the center of the flat, then tenting a thin piece of clear plastic over it, will get you close to the same effect.

The real trick is to keep them sunny and warm, no small feat in the Northeast winter. I now have 12-foot by 12-foot greenhouse I constructed from PVC pipe and clear plastic tarps, and I'll explain how to tackle that project in another book. It wasn't that long ago that I had to go old school. I have a large south-facing window in the main house that gets all sun most of the day, which can be as little as 8 hours in the winter, and the woodstove keeps the room around 70°, which are the two things you need to successfully sprout any seeds, especially onion seeds.

Much to the annoyance of my wife, I used a couple of scavenged plastic racks that you can find in most garages, and placed them directly in front of that window. I fitted the racks with small wheels so they can be moved around easily, and the rule of the house is if you pass by, you have to give the racks a quarter turn. By the end of the day, all sides have had some direct sun, and to play it safe, I covered the rack at night with clear plastic tarps in case the wood stove cools down. Gotta love that clear plastic tarp; it's got a million uses and the stuff is everywhere.

In the greenhouse, it can take 7 days for the onion seeds to sprout, and in the window it can take 10 to 12 days. I keep them covered and spritz them with the water bottle once a day to keep the moisture up until the sprouts reach about 3-4 inches high. At this point, I remove the cover and begin to water regularly, still being careful not to over-water. My goal is to get the seedlings up to transplant height of 5-6 inches, and, if timed right, this will be when spring is kissing the horizon.

As the temps begin to go above freezing, you're going to want to set your flats out so they can acclimate to the outside. Start off with a couple of hours a day for 3 to 4 days, and work your way up to all day. You want the sprouts to be standing up and a nice green from tip to stem. If they begin to droop and the tips begin to brown, you've gone too far and need to get them back into some warmth. You want them healthy, green, and acclimated so you can begin to transplant.

You are looking for the ground to be above freezing, I shoot for above 40 to 50°, and when the threat of an overnight frost is gone. I lay down an inch of mulch just to be on the safe side, and I remove the mulch from around the bulb as it matures.

The next important thing is planning, knowing where you're going to plant. Just like any other crop, you want to rotate where you plant, and if you want to use onions as a border crop (and I suggest you do), you need to know where your other crops are going. Onions don't play nice with peas and beans, but get along fine with peppers, tomatoes, and cabbage. As onions are going to be one of your first crops in, you need to have a full lay out to avoid any surprises.

I plant the seedlings an inch deep, keeping them 6-8 inches apart. For rows, I keep them a foot apart which gives me more than enough room for the bulbs to mature to good sizes. Remember, onions grow slow, but eat fast. Try to keep the ground damp until the bulbs begin to establish themselves, then you need to give the plants at least an inch of watering a week. For feeding, I use the compost tea every 3 weeks, and depending on the rain, I may bump that up to 2 weeks during the peak heat of the summer.

Sometimes Mother Nature can get confused and, for no reason that I can ever figure out, the onion will shoot up a seed stalk. There is no saving this; once the onion decides to go to seed, it's going to seed.

Once the seed stalk begins, all the energy goes to it and the onion loses its sweetness, and it's like the metabolism changes because the onion will not store well. Your best bet is to pick it and add it to that night's dinner.

HARVEST

You're looking at four months, a good 120 to 130 days, from transplant to harvest. What you are also looking for is all in the stem-like leaves, or tops, protruding from the bulb. These will not only tell you the health and size of the onion, but also if they are ready for harvest.

Onions grow in rings, and a medium-sized onion, which I personally feel is the perfect size, can have 4 to 5 rings. The trick to knowing how big your onions are is in fact no trick: each top represents a ring in the onion. If you see 2 or 3 tops, the onion will be on the small size; 4 to 5 tops, and you've got yourself a perfect medium-sized onion.

The tops will also play a major role in the harvest. As the bulb begins to reach the stage of maturity, it will be sending less energy to the tops and they will begin to fall over. I'm of the belief that once the tops begin to fall, the onion has done all it plans to do. When at least a third of the tops are down, I will gently push the rest down, trying to avoid snapping any of them. I will let them sit for at least three sunny days like this, because it allows the shock to subside and helps flick the switch for the curing to begin.

As with any of this stuff there are a number of tried and true ways to harvest onions: some pull up and lay out; some weave the tops and hang them; I leave them in place. It's more of a roll then a pull-up-- I roll the bulb up until the roots disconnect and are out of the ground, and then lay the onion on its side right where it grew, keeping the roots away from the ground. I will leave them to cure like this until the neck, where the top meets the bulb, begins to shrivel and the outer skin gets dry like paper. Some cut the tops off and use them like green onions, but personally I don't think they bring anything to the taste and texture table. I get more out of them in the compost than I do sprinkled on top my salad.

It may seem redundant or even stupid, but trust me letting the onion go through its phases of curing will pay off in the end. You can eat an onion right out of the ground, but it will be harsh and have more of a bite than a flavor. Allowing even a couple weeks of curing will mellow out the harshness, and turn the bite to a sweet taste. The curing allows the sugars to establish.

STORAGE

Onions keep well enough on their own to not need much in other forms of preserving. We use them in most dishes, so every jar of pickling and most sauces I put up have onion in them, and I also add sliced onion and garlic to every fifth jar or so of vegetables I can just to spice things up.

Occasionally, we get a fall crop of small onions that just don't want to mature. These range from 2-4 inches and normally will not keep well in dry storage. I keep them whole but peel the outer skin off, fill a sanitized mason jar with them, leaving a good inch of headspace, and add a teaspoon of salt. I fill the jar will hot water leaving a half-inch of headspace, seal with a sanitized lid and band, then process at 10 pounds pressure for 30 minutes.

These are great at the end of winter when stocks are running lean. They are good in soups, stews, and, of course, added to a pan of bacon and peas.

By far the best way to store these is in dry storage. As long as you took the time to cure and dry the onions during harvest, storing them is pretty simple. Some weave the tops and hang the onions from the rafters, others lay them out, and some bag them in netting. Whatever you choose, make sure there is enough air circulating to keep the onions dry. I use another item that is easily found almost everywhere, one of those things that looters ignored but has become quite handy: women's nylon stockings.

When it comes to onions these things are great. Depending on the size of both the stocking and onions, you can fit anywhere from 6 to 12 onions-- and in larger stockings up to 20. They stretch to fit, provide just enough air for good circulation, but still protect against insects. I cut out the bottom and tie it off with a loose knot and then roll the stocking down. I place two onions side by side, roll up the stocking just over the onion, place another one or two onions, roll up the stocking and repeat until the stocking is full. Keep in mind that gravity will be working against you, so don't overfill the stockings or you're going to find the onions laying on the floor feeding the field mice.

I hang these, knot side down, from the rafters of a shed that stays cool but never gets below freezing. As I need an onion or two, I untie the knot, let the onion fall out into my hands, and retie the knot. Gravity will push the rest down. I usually get only one season out of the nylons-- by the end of winter they get pretty stretched out and torn-- but they are easy to replace.

Versatile, medicinal, easy to grow, and damn tasty, onions are right up there with potatoes as an important post-apocalyptic food source.

ONION SOUP

Close to 90 percent of the recipes in these books have onion in the ingredients, and it was a challenge to pick any that highlighted the onion without taking away from another chapter. As I aim to please, I will offer the following for your culinary end-of-the-world pleasure, beginning with the all-time favorite onion soup, or French Onion Soup as they called it in the old world. Although, I do believe France doesn't exist anymore.

It's a good soup, and works well with those baby onions you canned and that leftover venison or beef stock you don't want to throw away.

What you'll need:

6 cups of beef, venison, or any red meat stock you have on hand (One time I had to substitute to make up the 6 cups and used 2 cups chicken stock, and if you have a chance to do this, I recommend it because it was damn good.)

4 large onions-- you can use the equivalent in the canned baby onions-- sliced thick to at least ¼ inch

Two slices of bacon (How many times do I have to tell you to get a bacon source?)

4 cloves of garlic, finely diced

1 bay leaf if you grow them, and you should

Salt and pepper to taste

Place the bacon in a large stock pot and slowly render out the fat until the bacon is crispy. Remove the bacon to crumble on top of the bowls later, or to eat now. Add the onion slices to the bacon fat and sauté on medium heat until they begin to brown. Add the garlic and bay leaf and continue to simmer, but avoid browning the garlic or it will add a bitter aftertaste. You want to keep the sauté moving until the onions take on a golden color. Add the stock, cover, and simmer another 30 minutes.

Depending on your food stocks, an added bonus would be to turn a bowl over onto a piece of bread, slice the excess bread sticking out from under the bowl so that you have a piece that fits snugly inside the bowl. Toast the bread until brown on both sides, fill the bowl with the onion soup and top the bowl with the bread. If you make your own or have bartered some cheese, shred and top the bowl off with it. Place in the oven for 1 to 2 minutes so the cheese is melted.

This is a belly-filling bowl of awesome that you don't mind is meatless.

BAKED ONION

The surest sign that spring is around the corner and winter's beginning to loosen its grip on the land; mornings are still cold, but the days are not as cold and your food stocks and wood pile are getting low. When the pickings begin to get slim and you're trying to stretch leftovers, this is a good dish, side dish, light lunch, just all-around something good to eat.

What you'll need:

4 medium-to-large onions, peeled but kept whole

½ to 1 cup of water, depending on the pot

1 cup of whatever leftover meat you have on hand, beef, chicken, pork, or game, finely diced (The only thing that doesn't work well with this is fish, although I've never tried this with shellfish.)

4 slices of bacon (Do I need to repeat myself?)

2 to 3 large cloves of garlic, finely diced

1 Teaspoon of Italian seasoning (That recipe will be in the herb and spice book. For now, some finely-chopped oregano, sage, rosemary and parsley will do.)

½ cup bread crumbs

Salt and pepper to taste

Cut both ends off the onions and peel the outer layer off, but keep the onion whole. In a medium-sized pot, pour in the water so that it's about an inch deep, and place the onions standing up inside. Cover and put on medium heat for ten to twenty minutes. What you're looking for is to steam, more than cook, the onion, but you don't want to cook the onions through. You want the onions to just begin to soften, but still have some resistance if you push a knife into them.

Remove the onions from the pot, but do not throw away that water, and let the onions cool for the next steps-- it just makes them easier to handle. When they're at room temperature, I use a soup spoon and begin gently digging out the top of the onions, holding them firmly, but not squeezing. I'm looking for a width of the spoon, and trying for 2/3 deep into the onions.

I dice up the part of the onion that was scooped out and add to the diced protein, diced garlic, and season and mix all together. This mixture gets spooned back into the cavity of the onions, loosely-packed because it may expand during baking. Wrap each onion with a slice of bacon, top off with the bread crumbs, and place in a deep baking pan uncovered, unless you're using a Dutch oven over an open fire. You want to bake these at medium heat, 350°, until the mixture is cooked. On average, you're looking at 30 to 45 minutes, and you want the mixture to be fully cooked but not dry, the bacon not overly crispy, and the onion soft.

You could just eat them as is, but I always like to go the next level. I add the onion water, 1 clove of diced garlic, a pinch of the Italian seasoning, and a teaspoon of the bacon fat to a cup of beef or chicken broth, depending on what protein you used, and boil this until it reduces to a thick glaze. Then, spoon the glaze over the tops of the onion just before serving.

Sitting by the fire on a cold evening, a plate of baked stuffed onion, glass of homemade wine, and a new book you scavenged from an abandoned house you just found... good times after the world went to shit.

ONION FRY BREAD

What else can I say? Fry bread is good. It's easy to make, works with just about anything, and allows you to once again use that dreaded powdered milk in a good way. The only problem I can see is that it may be an issue for some because of the ingredients, but look at this as a challenge for your next scavenging trip.

What you'll need:

1 medium onion, finely diced

1 cup of flour

¼ teaspoon salt

1 teaspoon powdered milk

1 teaspoon of baking powder (To be honest this has never been one of those items that has been difficult to find. No one looks for it or thinks it will come in handy when they see it. I've never come back from a trip without at least a couple of cans of this stuff.)

½ cup water

Cooking oil for frying

Sift all dry ingredients into a large bowl. I have a nifty 4-cup sifter with a hand trigger that does a great job, but a fine-meshed screen in a wooden frame will do just as well. The key is to sift, not mix, as you want all the ingredients, especially the small clumps of baking powder, well-incorporated. Flour your hands well to keep the dough from sticking and begin to work in the water. This you want to mix, not knead, or you'll make the dough tough, and mix only until all the ingredients are incorporated and formed into a ball. Cover with a damp cloth and let it rest at least half an hour.

Cut the dough into four parts. Spread a fourth of the diced onion on the table and roll the dough in the onion. Then using your fingers, you want to both stretch and pull the dough into a flat round shape the size of a large saucer, like the ones you use for your soup bowls. The trick is trying to embed as much of the diced onion into and onto the dough as you stretch.

While you are stretching, you should begin to heat your oil. I use a deep cast-iron pan that I fill with an inch or so of oil, and let the oil get hot enough to fry. Two ways to check this is drop a small piece of dough into the oil; if it begins to cook immediately, then the oil is ready. A second way is to lay a wooden spoon on top of the oil, and if bubbles appear along the edge of the spoon, then the oil is ready.

Place the stretched dough into the oil and fry for 3 to 4 minutes per side. What you're looking for is a golden brown; the dough should puff up a bit so don't freak, its fry bread not flat bread.

ODDS AND ENDS

Compost tea. I couldn't honestly tell you how much of this stuff I go through in a season-- gallons of it, I suppose. I always have a container brewing, and when I strain that, I automatically begin another. I mean, why not, you're not wasting anything. The strained compost can go right back into your compost pile, and any tea left over can go right into the raised beds before your final tilling and compost for the winter.

What you'll need:

Five-gallon bucket with lid

Enough aged compost to half-fill a five-gallon bucket

Enough water, rain water works well, to fill the rest of the five-gallon bucket, and also dilute the tea afterwards

A long stirrer

Cloth, drying screen, or some type of fine mesh to strain the compost

The recipe is very simple: half-fill the five-gallon bucket with good, aged compost. Add water until the bucket is full, leaving a 4-inch headspace which makes it easier and less messy to stir. You want to cover and let the tea steep for at least 7 days (although, it doesn't go bad if you leave it longer), stirring it 2 to 3 times a day. When ready, you'll want to strain the tea into another bucket.

How you plan to distribute this will dictate how well you should strain. If you plan on using some sort of ladle to spoon the tea around the plant, then don't worry too much about compost sediment after you strain. If you plan on using a hand-pump garden sprayer, then I would suggest a couple of strains through a finer mesh to avoid sediment clogging the device.

To use, you still need to dilute the tea to prevent any root damage. I use a 1:10 ratio of 1 part tea to 10 parts water. Also remember you're feeding the ground first, which in turn will feed the plant, so do not spray the plant directly; instead, ladle or spray around the base of the plant. On average, I feed the garden every two weeks during the peak growing season.

GARLIC

While garlic is good at warding off vampires, I've learned the infected have no sense of smell, so I'm shit out of luck with that. Not only is garlic a main source of flavor to your food, but it has become an important medicinal herb in these post-apocalyptic times. In addition to helping reduce heart disease by lowering blood cholesterol levels, it also boosts the immune system by helping the body with the defenses to fight off bacterial and viral infections.

Some of the old remedies that have returned include using garlic to treat a toothache. Simply apply crushed garlic to the infected tooth; it will burn at first, but the ache in tooth will soon disappear. Repeat this over the course of a couple of days and the infection should disappear. Before going to bed, rub some crushed garlic on a wart and cover with a bandage. Then twice during the day, rub garlic juice on the wart, and within a few weeks the wart should diminish. It has been said the same treatment can be used on acne.

Making a garlic tea of just boiling water and a couple cloves of garlic can help with that annoying cough. Drink the tea after it has simmered a few minutes and it will not only help open your nasal passages so you can breathe better, it will also alleviate the itchiness from that post-nasal drip that is causing you to cough. No one is going to want to talk to or kiss you for the better part of the day, but you will feel better.

One section you will not see here is the seeding section. I know garlic seeds exist, but I've never seen any. When there was such a thing as Google, I did learn that garlic seeds are very small, black, and not unlike onion seeds. I also learned that seeding a garlic bulb can be near impossible, and if you do manage to get a seed stalk to grow, the flowers of the seed head die off long before the seeds have had time to develop. What really turned me away from exploring this any further was the information that told me if I was to get my hands on some seeds, growing garlic from seed can take upwards of three years for a bulb to develop, if it develops at all.

My goal here was to make this as simple and as uncomplicated as possible, and a growth period of three years with a possibility of nothing to show for it at the end is not my idea of simple and uncomplicated. So I'm not going to waste our time on the seeding process. I've always planted garlic by the clove, and that is what I show here.

PRE-PLANTING

I've been growing garlic from cloves since before the crash of humanity, so I have never had the challenge of having to find garlic bulbs. I will say most produce vendors in the new villages will have garlic and will barter them off, and I suggest you make the initial sacrifice and obtain a couple bulbs. It's a safe bet you will be able to replace whatever you bartered fairly quickly, and the couple of bulbs you get for your troubles realistically could feed your family indefinitely. The garlic my family is eating today can be directly connected to the cloves I planted over ten years ago. Keep in mind garlic is one of those long-growth, eat-fast kind of plants. Kind of like having a teenager around, it seems they will never grow up and always want to eat. They also need a good month or more of temperatures below 40° to mature properly, because there's something about a cold snap that flicks the switch on bulb development. Without this cold period, the plant will still grow, but at harvest time you could end up with a thick green stalk on top and a marble-sized clove on the bottom. On the other side of the spectrum, as temperatures get close to 80°, the bulb will slow down or stop its growth.

For me, this means a fall planting-- I aim for the first two weeks of October which should give me a harvest by mid-to-late July. Again, this will mean some long-term planning because the bed I use for the fall planting is dedicated to the garlic for the entire following spring season. The other challenge is to not use a bed that you used for garlic, or any other onion plants the previous season. To do so could increase the chances of passing on pests or disease. I do also use garlic as a border crop, but these I plant very early in the spring. Although I can get in enough cold to initiate bulb growth with a shortened grow time, and the fact I push these into July and sometimes August, it usually gives me smaller bulbs. I find this an acceptable trade-off. I still add garlic to my food stocks, and help protect my other crops from garlic-hating pests.

PLANTING

After each year's harvests, I set aside the largest, best-looking bulbs for the next season's planting. There is no mystery, no tricks, and no experience necessary. I take the bulbs, break them apart, and sort the cloves by size. I don't make a big deal about the paper-like skin around the cloves, I don't make any effort to remove them or keep them on-- it will not make a difference in the outcome either way.

OK guys, that age-old question has been answered: size really does matter, at least when it comes to garlic cloves. Again, I will not bore you with the botanist science babble as to why, but if you plant the larger, outer cloves you will get larger bulbs, while the inner, smaller cloves will produce smaller bulbs. Frankly, I don't think it matters at the end of the day. When your movements are restricted because of three feet of snow on the ground, and with winter storms raging every couple of days, are you really going to be concerned that one garlic bulb is slightly smaller than the other? I may avoid using the small cloves for border crops which already produce a smaller bulb, but other than that, I will use most of the bulb, saving the ultra-small center cloves for that night's dinner.

Because the raised bed is tilled down to at least two feet, planting the cloves is pretty straight forward. I just push the clove down about 2 inches deep with the tip of the clove pointing up, no fuss or complicated directions. I keep the cloves at least 6 inches apart in rows at least 12 inches apart, which helps with weeding. I also experience an extended period of below-freezing weather, so I top the bed with at least 6 inches of mulch. I would suggest heavy mulching even in warmer climates to protect against a surprise frost, and to keep the ground damp. New cloves need moisture to develop their roots, but over-watering will stunt and even rot the clove. I also give the bed a good spray of Compost Tea to get the cloves through the winter months.

Caring for garlic plants is not that difficult either, as long as you keep an eye on the water levels. Once again, use the best measuring tool all of you have: your finger. If the ground is dry, give it a watering. My rule of thumb during early to mid-spring is to give the bed a heavy watering once a week if it hasn't rained. As the temps begin to rise, I will hold back on the watering, letting the ground stay on the dry side of the scale. As the bulbs begin to develop, I will feed them once every couple of weeks and I will also, using that trusty old finger of mine, loosen the soil around the developing bulbs.

By the end of spring into the beginning of summer, a center stalk will begin to shoot out of the center of the bulb. If left alone, this stalk, or as some call them scapes, will begin to curl around itself and produce a seed head at the top of it. As I wrote before, at best it is difficult to get seeds to fully mature, and if accomplished, growing from seed is a long and frustrating affair. In addition, the scapes will divert most of the plant's energy to the seed bulb and away from the developing garlic bulb. By far the deciding vote on what to do is the fact that the scapes are not only very edible, but actually are very good.

Without guilt, as soon as the scape begins to curl I pinch it off at the base, dice it up, and add it to either a salad or stir-fry for that night's dinner.

HARVESTING

By mid-to-late summer begin to loosen the soil around the bulb to help them grow larger. As late summer hits the tips of the leaves will begin to dry and turn brown. I harvest when most of the tips have dried, as leaving the bulbs too long in the ground can cause the bulb to split the individual cloves apart, and once the cloves begin to split, the bulb will not store well.

Because I have kept the soil around the bulbs loose, I usually have no problems lifting the bulbs out of the ground by grabbing at the neck where the leaves meet the bulb and gently pulling up. If I feel any resistance at all, I will use a garden trowel to loosen the soil around the bulb. Never force the bulb out; garlic bulbs bruise easily and the cloves can break apart, and-- again-- damaged bulbs will not store well.

I have a spot in the yard that gets some sun in the morning and late afternoon, but shade most of the day. This is the perfect spot to lay out the garlic for a couple of days to let the outer skin of the bulb dry out. If there is a chance for rain, move the bulbs inside. Rain or too much sun can damage the outer skin, and that skin is the first defense needed for long-term storage.

STORAGE

Like onions, storing garlic is easy and pretty straight forward. Doesn't matter if you trim down the leaves and store in a mesh bag, or braid the leaves to hang. The few things you want to do is make sure none of the bulbs show bruising or damage, and you want to feel the bulbs to insure the individual cloves have not become loose. Any of these things can invite disease and rot, which can spread quickly when stored closely to other bulbs.

I don't wash the bulbs before storing because I want to avoid bruising and damaging the outer skin. After the bulbs have been left to dry for a couple of days, I will take a soft brush and gently brush away any dried dirt. I'll do this six bulbs at a time and then braid them, but there is no real mandate on how to braid. Some like to be fancy because they will hang the garlic in their kitchen and it becomes an edible art. Others, like me, just overlap the leaves as we line the bulbs on top of each other. You want to hang these away from direct sunlight, and in a spot that is dry.

If you have the luxury of owning a supply of mesh bags, then at the point of harvest you want to trim the roots off and cut back the leaves to about an inch or two from the bulb just before laying out to dry. The trick with the mesh is you still want the bulbs in a single row to allow full air circulation, otherwise if the bulbs bunch up to the bottom, the bulbs could face some rot in the long term.

Regardless of which of these two methods of storage you use, you want to let the new harvest cure for two to three weeks. Of course, you can eat the cloves right out of the ground, but you will notice the flavor has a sharper edge to it. After 3 to 4 weeks of curing, that sharpness will mellow into that garlic flavor we all know and love.

For those of you looking for more options of preserving, I will strongly suggest you don't store garlic in oil, or try to can in your pressure cooker. I know some of you remember jars of diced garlic in water and oil that were safely sold in stores. These were professionally preserved in machines that could raise the temperatures in excess of 250° quickly to kill any bacteria without affecting the texture and flavor of the garlic. The pressure canner you have may just reach 250°, but the time and pressures needed will turn any cloves or dice into an unpleasant mush.

You can safely pickle and dry cloves, and I have recipes for these to follow, but I personally don't see a need for any other process. If bulbs are handled correctly, you can get a 6 to 8 month shelf-life out of them, and that should get you close to the next harvest. Why play with the health of you and yours?

GARLIC POWDER

This is so simple you're going to kick your dog. OK, that was not as funny as it was bouncing around in my head, but the process is simple. This is perfect in the fall for those small cloves you didn't want to plant, or in the summer for any bulbs that may have gotten damaged. Yet, the bigger question is: why dry?

It is a safe way to preserve, but you're paying a price with a loss of texture and some flavor. However, there are some major gains including storage, versatility, and in some dishes, powder seems to work better. To me, garlic toast tastes better with a sprinkle of garlic powder, rather than scraping a clove across the bread. I think the powder works well in mashed potatoes and most salads. My biggest argument in favor of drying garlic is that it travels easily.

Some of my trading and scavenging trips can keep me from the homestead for a couple of days, and without gas-powered engines, you have to learn how to travel as lightly as possible. I have a horse-and-buggy, but even so, traveling is long and hard enough without having to over pack-- and bulky jars of seasonings are out of the question. When it comes to food, much of it I will try to hunt on the road, and to have a small pouch of a mixture of onion and garlic powder and Italian seasonings to dress the game is like a taste of home.

What you'll need:

Garlic, sliced in half

Sheet pan or flat pan

A drying source

The most complicated step to this process is finding the right drying source. If you're going with the indirect heat of a stove, you need to make sure the oven can maintain a steady 150° for 4 to 6 hours. There is a major difference between drying and cooking, and if your stove requires a lot of attention to maintain heat, this may not be a good source for drying. Once the heat rises above 250°, the cloves will begin to cook, and the end results will be more of a garlic paste then a powder.

I have a friend in the next village who has an old car at the back of his field that gets full sun all day. In summer, he will lay whatever he is drying on a sheet pan and place the pan on the dashboard of the car. He cracks the windows open to regulate the heat, but the solar effect through the windshield will dry out the tray within a day. I've used this same method with a cold frame that had an old storm window on top. Depending on time of year and the strength of the sun, it can take a bit longer, but the solar method allows you to set and forget.

Whichever method you choose, you want to lay the sliced cloves evenly on the tray, not having the slices touch. You're looking for an end result of the cloves becoming dry and almost brittle to the touch, with a golden color.

To grind, you can use mortar and pestle, just smooth out a bowl shape into a flat stone and make a handle with a rounded end out of some hard wood-- you will be surprised at how well they work. I, on the other hand, like to take the lazy man's way out with a hand grinder. I have a number of them I use for different purposes because the flavors can carry over. In small batches I will rough grind, then set the grinder down a notch and repeat. I will do this until I get the fine powder I'm looking for. I store these in mason jars and they will keep for up to 6 months, but I have also used some forgotten powder that was just over a year old, and it tasted fine.

ODDS AND ENDS

All this writing got me to thinking about the old days. There wasn't much left from those times, but I did find a box of some of my letters and postings. The one I share here I had posted on a survival website before the crash, and I think best describes my mindset in those times.

Why all the Bug-out bags?

The issue I have with the Prepper and Survival Movement of recent is the lack of sustainable and homesteading skills. There seems to be a heavy lean towards hoarding goods and wilderness survival, and granted, while these skills are important, they will not provide one of the most fundamental needs each and every one of us will look for after a SHTF occurrence happens. These skills will help you survive, but they will not help you live.

Let's throw an example out there for all of us to toy with. I'm not a big fan of reality shows, but one that aired over the summer caught my attention. The premise was simple enough: men with various survival experiences were placed in the wilderness with limited supplies. The goal was to be the last person standing and win a cash prize. The show, in my opinion, correctly highlighted the stresses that trying to "just survive" puts on the mind, body, and soul. As experienced as some were, by month three, nine contestants had physically and emotionally cracked in one way or another.

This brings me to my point of debate. While we are preparing to survive, we need to also learn the old school ways on how to live. Your survival training has taught you to set snares for small game, but what do you do when you catch something? The added stresses on your loved ones watching you hack away at a rabbit is something neither you nor they need. Of course, field-dressing a wild animal may be something that is out of your reach right now, but there are other ways to practice this.

Next time you're shopping for groceries, bypass the packages of wings and boneless and skinless chicken breasts, and buy a whole bird. It's a safe bet that the internet has a video you can follow, but practice skinning, quartering, and deboning the chicken. After a few times of doing this and when you're feeling comfortable, move up to a turkey. Practice taking the bird carcass, along with the cut ends of vegetables that you normally throw away, and add water to make a stock out of it. Do the same for fish, by whole and scale, skin and filet it yourself. Take the bones, fins, and head, and practice making fish stock.

The same goes for vegetables. It doesn't matter what your current living conditions are; you should be growing something. A pot of tomatoes and hanging pots of herbs on the balcony; some five-gallon buckets with tomatoes, peppers, and potatoes in a sunny corner of the yard the landlord gave you the ok to use; or a bigger garden in your own backyard. It doesn't matter what it is, or where you are: always have something edible growing. The only rule I offer is to grow what you and your family like and will eat. If no one in your family likes peppers, then why waste the time or the growing space?

Even though you don't need to store food for the winter, practice doing so anyways. Invest $100 or so to get a basic pressure cooker and rack of mason jars. When the supermarket has a sale involving produce, get what you can afford and practice canning what you're not going to eat right away.

Grow, dry, and grind your own spice blends. Look at the ingredients of the blends and rubs you and your family enjoy, and order these seeds to grow them. In most cases, these ingredients can be growing year-round in hanging pots in your window. Practice drying: it can be as simple as hanging the herbs in a dry spot. The real trick will be grinding the right blend, as not all rubs have equal amounts of each ingredient, and finding the right combination will take some time and a bit of eating.

The difference between a carcass speared by a stick and cooked over an open flame, and a well-seasoned piece of meat served on a plate with a side of fresh vegetables, can be the difference between emotional survival and total breakdown.

When I started, I would begin on the Monday after Thanksgiving and only use, except for meat, what I was able to store or can through the summer and fall until that was all used up. Not only did this save me a crapload of money in groceries, it also gave me an idea of how much I would need to get through an average winter.

The overall point here is none of us can truly prepare for the immense stresses that a disaster will dump onto us, and it is those stresses that will cause the most damage and hardships to survivors. One of the surest ways to offset this is to have a plan that goes beyond survival, and includes creating a sustainable life for you and yours. There is no better way to do this than with a home-cooked meal with fresh food.

A MAN AND HIS FAMILY

The man placed the manuscript down on the box-- the same box the stranger left going on eight months ago, and upended as it was, the box was the perfect height for an end table of sorts. He thought it was fitting that the box should now take the place of honor in his spot next to his chair inside his home.

He sat back in the rocker scratching at his beard, now clean and fairly trimmed, and he let the thought roll around in his mind for a moment.

Inside his home.

Last spring, starved, weak, and worn down by the harsh winter, he had all but given up. He was convinced he would be dead within a couple months, and his wife and son not long after. Then the stranger arrived with the box, and the box helped save them from the fingers of death that were quickly squeezing close around them. It was the box, or all that was in it, that brought them from the brink of barely living in a shack, to a healthier and cleaner life in what he felt was becoming a home.

At first glance, a person may not think much of what he done to the place, but he knew it was miles away from what it had been just a few months before. At the time, it was more of a shack than a cabin. The gaps between the outside wooden slats that last year allowed the cold wind free passage inside were now filled with a mixture of mud, straw, and moss. On the inside, in between the studs, he layered scavenged cardboard and then covered the walls with sheets of clear plastic that he seemed to find everywhere. It was not much to look at, he would agree, but it has kept the crisp fall wind out so far, and it was keeping in the heat from the wood stove.

They will not be cold or wet this winter.

If he can help it, they won't be hungry either. With the seeds from the box, he has been able to put up over 50 pounds of potatoes, 30 pounds of carrots, and over 30 bulbs of onions. He also found a small, abandoned village about half a day's walk to the west where he was able to scavenge dry rice, dry beans, flour, and enough canned goods to more than last until next year's harvest.

On one trip, he brought back a pressure canner and a cartload of pint and quart-sized jars. His wife was able to use this to put up 18 quarts of tomato sauce, 10 quarts of whole tomatoes, and a dozen or so pints of string beans, peas and even pickles. No, they would not be cold or hungry this winter.

He looked over to his son sitting at the table they made from sawhorses and plywood. The boy was shaving down a long stick to make into an arrow for the long bow the man had found on his last trip to the village. The boy, dressed in hemmed up jeans and a clean blue flannel shirt that was a bit bulky on his small frame, has gotten quite good at catching rabbits and other small game, and was determined to use the bow to get a turkey for Thanksgiving.

On the other side of the large open room, his wife was stirring the stew pot that was eagerly bubbling on top of the wood stove. She, too, was dressed in jeans and bulky red flannel, all brought back from the

village. Her hair, now thickly streaked in gray, was rolled into a bun on the back of her head, while the near-death from last year has left its mark of deep creases along her forehead and around her eyes. The creases didn't matter to him; she had pushed forward and worked just as hard as he to get ready for the winter, all without complaint.

The smells from the pot triggered a grumble from deep in his gut. He knew the rabbit they caught this morning was skinned, quartered, and now dancing with some diced potatoes, carrots, and onions in its own gravy. Life was differently getting better, and all because of the stranger and his box.

He leaned back with closed eyes. The other preparations he wanted to get done before the snow and cold came knocking at his door were flashing in his mind for attention, but he was also thinking of next spring already. Thinking of the new planting, resuming trips to the abandoned village next year, maybe for furniture or materials for real walls. A smile began to spread across his lips; he was thinking of what lay in the future for him and his family.

The future. Last year, he was waiting to die, and now he is thinking of the future. His thoughts now too crowded, he opened his eyes and reached into the box for the manuscript labeled *Zombie Gardener: Book Two*, figuring he should get some reading in before dinner.

END

ABOUT THE AUTHOR

John Barry first came in contact with the Zombie Gardener through what he called the magic of science and some damn good pharmaceuticals. He said he couldn't tell if it was the new pain meds the doctor gave him for his knees, the amazing pot his wife scored, or some questionable mushrooms he found in the back yard. What he can tell you is something happened that night that allowed a form of communication across dimensions, or time, or Dr. Who-style space travel.

The best way John describes Z's communication is that Z's the voice inside his head. A voice described as deep and smooth like a grandfather's pipe smoke. John's just happy that he can now communicate without moving his lips.

John, his wife Debbie and their dog Maggie live a simple life in the outskirts of Brockton, Mass surrounded by family and friends. All are quietly awaiting the apocalypse.

Made in the USA
Columbia, SC
15 September 2019